Research Priorities in North-East India

With Special Reference to Assam

R. Gopalakrishnan

2021

Regency Publications

A Division of

Astral International Pvt. Ltd.

New Delhi – 110 002

First Published, 2001

Reprinted, 2021

ISBN: 9788187498414

Published by : **Regency Publications**
A Division of
Astral International Pvt. Ltd.
– ISO 9001:2015 Certified Company –
4736/23, Ansari Road, Darya Ganj
New Delhi-110 002
Ph. 011-43549197, 23278134
E-mail: info@astralint.com
Website: www.astralint.com

Foreword

In the year 1992–93, the ICSSR-North-Eastern Regional Centre, Shillong, planned to sponsor one day panel discussions on Research Priorities in the Seven States of North-East India, sometimes also referred to as the seven sisters, namely Arunachal Pradesh, Assam, Manipur, Meghalaya, Mizoram, Nagaland and Tripura. Of these seven states Assam is the largest in terms of both area and population. It was, therefore, rightly thought that a single one day panel discussion may not do justice to the research priorities in Social Sciences for a large state like Assam. Hence, it was decided to hold three panel discussions in three different and widely apart cities and towns of Assam.

The choice of Dibrugarh and Gauhati in the Brahmaputra Valley, and Karimganj in the Barak Valley was considered most appropriate in view of the socio-cultural divergence of the regions represented by the respective towns. Prof. Atul Goswami of the Department of Economics, Dibrugarh University, Dibrugarh and Prof. A.C. Bhagabati of the Institute of Social Change and Development (now known as OKD as Institute of Social Change and De elopment) Gauhati, and Dr. Apurbananda Mazumdar of the Department of History, R.S. Girls College, Karimganj, were requested to organise the panel discussions and coordinate them.

All the aforesaid scholars accepted our request and invited a number of locally available scholars in different fields of Social Science to prepare an article on Research Priorities in their subject and to participate in the panel discussions. Consequently, Prof. Atul Goswami held the panel discussion on May 25, 1992, at Disbrugarh, and Dr. Apurbananda Mazumdar held it on May 28, 1992 at Karimganj. These two panel discussions were followed a little later by another at Gauhati. Prof. A.C. Bhagabati held it on March 13, 1993.

Needless to say that all the three panel discussions were well attended and successful on all counts. Participants discussed the papers and identified the priority areas of research in different Social Science disciplines. We take this opportunity to thank Professors Atul Goswami, A.C. Bhagabati and Dr. Apurbananda Mazumdar and their friends and colleagues who contributed to make these discussions academically fruitful.

Prof. R. Gopalakrishnan is a senior scholar and Social Scientist of the region known for his scholarly contributions both within the region and beyond the region. I am thankful to him for having accepted our offer to edit this volume of the Research Priorities, and completing the work right on time. I must also thank our Deputy Director, Dr. C.J. Thomas, for his interest in the research priorities without whose help and co-operation it would not have been possible to bring out these volumes.

I hope that this series on Research Priorities on North-East India in general, and Assam in particular, will be useful to all those interested in the researches on the North-Eastern parts of the country.

Shillong
July, 2001

Jai Prakash Singh
Ex. Hon. Director
ICSSR-NERC

Preface

This is a collection of papers presented by Research on Assam. This was essentially a local level panel discussion, which after a serious deliberation came out with definite recommendations. This effort is, therefore, to present the findings. These findings are preceded by a background of the current status of the State of Assam and is followed by identification and priorities of research for the state in the twenty-first century.

This work has been initiated at the behest of the North-Eastern regional Centre—ICSSR, Shillong, which is actively pursuing its effort to promote, sponsor and publish research priorities in the North-Eastern Region of India. The present section highlights research priorities for the state of Assam.

I extend my sense of appreciation to the Honorary Director Prof. J.P. Singh, and Deputy Director Dr C.J. Thomas, for providing the opportunity to associate myself with this volume. I also express my sense of appreciation to Ms. C. Khonglah and other staff of the office of the NERC-ICSSR, for their assistance and co-operation in completing this assignment. Last but not the least, I acknowledge my appreciation to Dr. N.P. Goel for bringing this manuscript in the final form.

Prof. R. Gopalakrishnan
Editor

Contents

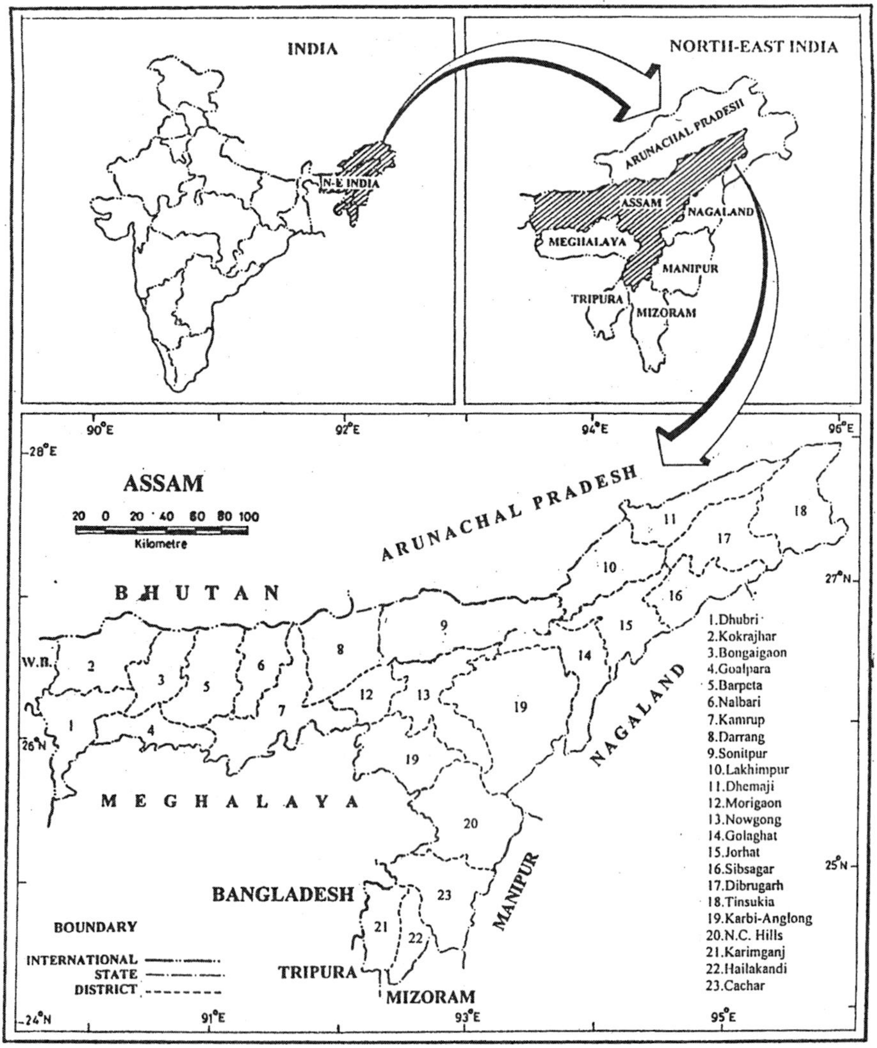
INDIA
N-E INDIA
NORTH-EAST INDIA
ARUNACHAL PRADESH
ASSAM
NAGALAND
MEGHALAYA
MANIPUR
TRIPURA
MIZORAM
ASSAM
20 0 20 40 60 80 100
Kilometre
BHUTAN
ARUNACHAL PRADESH
W.B.
MEGHALAYA
BANGLADESH
NAGALAND
MANIPUR
TRIPURA
MIZORAM
BOUNDARY
INTERNATIONAL
STATE
DISTRICT
90°E
92°E
94°E
96°E
91°E
93°E
95°E
28°E
27°N
26°N
25°N
24°N
1.Dhubri
2.Kokrajhar
3.Bongaigaon
4.Goalpara
5.Barpeta
6.Nalbari
7.Kamrup
8.Darrang
9.Sonitpur
10.Lakhimpur
11.Dhemaji
12.Morigaon
13.Nowgong
14.Golaghat
15.Jorhat
16.Sibsagar
17.Dibrugarh
18.Tinsukia
19.Karbi-Anglong
20.N.C. Hills
21.Karimganj
22.Hailakandi
23.Cachar

Introduction

This book, Research Priorities in North-East India (with special reference to Assam), has attempted to identify the research priorities in a state that has indicated sizeable conflict situations. It is also apparent that if such an effort is indeed made, it will pave way for a better understanding of the problems facing the state and perhaps add to the competence in resolving as much of the conflicts as possible. Above all, the present attempt is an effort to place these research priorities in a contemporary perspective and as an alternative to the all too common approach to the problems of the state.

Even after five decades of Independence, the North-East India in general and the state of Assam in particular, continues to attract scant attention from scholars, administrators and policy-makers. It is only in the recent past that the concern for the region's status has been expressed. In more than one way, this apathy has been encouraged by social and economic stagnation. This has led to instability to dominate the regional transactions and relations. It has also encouraged mushrooming of political fora and militant organisations that reflected the revolutionary changes in the perception of the protagonists in the region. The experiences of stagnating economy, inadequate communication infrastructure and frequently ineffective relief, remedial and growth mechanisms have abetted this. These have undermined socio-cultural and economic fabric of the society. So that, today the region and the state in particular is at the crossroads of consolidation and growth on the one hand, and stagnation and political instability on the other.

In fact, the phenomena of social and political relations has encouraged examination of some of the socio-economic instances. But despite the interest, which has been created by this problem, there is a limited literature. Those who have written the bulk of material on the state and the region, have prepared it with a professional interest on the subject of socio-political instability. These were meant for professional audience. At the wider levels of regional development, the deliberations on the present theme have been conducted at levels totally inadequate to assess and formulate policies for development of the state (and the region).

Assam is a miniature replica of the Indian Sub-continent. Its geography has the characteristics that enabled many of the trans-regional elements to adopt themselves to the meso-level ecological conditions of the Brahmaputra-Barak system or the Assam. So that, it's history, is one of continuous reflections of large-scale population movements, where each cultural strain while maintaining its exclusiveness, coexisted with others. These migratory population streams used the plain and valley section of the North-East as a transit point—a staging point for empire formation or only to settle in the adjoining hill and mountain territories. Be that as it may, the state gradually witnessed transition from a primitive economy to a subsistence economy, with every population wave adding to the technology and change.

Over a period of time, these development enabled development of agrarian economy that was self-sustaining. These were the forerunners of elements that were conducive for formation of states and military-feudal structures in the valley landscape. In each historical period, there was constant struggle for space and confrontation over the control of subsistence between the original inhabitants, the colonisers, the immigrants and the conquerors—rulers. These became the basis on which all-subsequent historical geographical transactions of exclusiveness of space by the concerned population groups and subgroups were based.

In fact, the historical patterns were responsible for marginalisation of many peoples in the region. However, these processes induced plural structures and relationships to emerge and dominate the regional landscape. Regional variations, differences, disparities and inequalities, remained latent but had the potential to translate a peaceful landscape to an unstable political entity. Interacting with the regional geopolitical compulsions, participation and representation became the most common theme on which competition over space, confrontation over the control of means and conflicts over management were based. These became all the more imperative, when change and modernisation had horizontally and vertically divided the society. It is, in keeping with this perspective, that the present study has been undertaken.

Location

The state of Assam is situated in the extreme North-Eastern part of the country. It lies, between 24°8′N latitude and 87°42′E and 96°E longitude. Assam forms the core of the North-Eastern region, (comprising the states of Arunachal Pradesh, Manipur, Meghalaya, Mizoram, Nagaland and Tripura, besides Assam). It is bound by the states of Arunachal Pradesh in the north and North-East; by Nagaland and Manipur in the east; by the states of Mizoram and Tripura in the south-east; by Meghalaya in the south; and by West Bengal in the west. It has international boundaries with Bangladesh in the south-east and south-west and with Bhutan in the north and North-East. The state has Goalpara in the lower Brahmaputra valley and Cachar in the Barak valley as the gateways to the state and the North-East region itself. The significance of these gateways lay in their historical role in transforming relationships and transactions of the region. The entire region is connected with the rest of India by a slender corridor leading from Dhubri and Kokrajhar districts of Assam—the Siliguri Neck.

Assam has a geographical area of 78,438 sq. km. or 78.438,000 ha. This is 2.4 percent of the total geographical area of the country. The state comprises of two major river regimes of the Brahmaputra and the Barak of the Meghna systems. In other words, there are two distinct natural regions, viz., the plain area of the Brahmaputra and the Barak valleys comprising of twenty-one districts. The districts in the plains are Dhubri, Bongaigaon, Kokrajhar, Goalpara, Barpeta, Nalbari, Kamrup, Darrang, Sonitpur, Lakhimpur, Dhemaji, Dibrugarh, Tinsukia, Sibsagar, Jorhat, Golaghat, Nagaon, Morigaon, Karimganj Hailakandi and Cachar; and the hill areas consisting of the two hill districts of Karbi Anglong and North Cachar

Hills (have their own autonomous district Councils), cover an area of 15,200 sq. km and accounts for about a fifth of the land area of the state. The state has a population of 22,294,562 persons (1991 Census). Of this population, 6.24 percent is in the category of Scheduled Caste and 10.99 percent in the category of Scheduled Tribe population. With an average density of 284 persons per Square Kilometre, highest density is found in the district of Dhubri (467) and lowest in the district of North Cachar Hills (30). The State in the 1971–91 period averaged a growth rate of 52.44 percent. This growth is higher than the national average and has out stripped the rate of economic development.

Historical Outline

Major river basins of the state experienced separate historical development. From the available literature, one can easily discern that the Brahmaputra valley with its insular characteristics displayed prominent South-East Asian influences while the Barak Valley, located in the south-eastern extremity of the Indo-Ganga plains in the east, indicated profound deltaic influences. Accessibility, through the mountain passes located in the eastern adjoining territories and the continuous stretch of flat lands, permitted settlement and movement across the valley. Regional ecological conditions modified the requirements for adaptation. These were conducive for the development of individual elements. These established broad regional trends and alignments that laid the foundation of the valley societies. All these societies were characterised by several layers of identity with varying cultural backgrounds. The coming together of this amalgam brought about significant fusion of socio-cultural elements to provide a basis for a plural society. These affected the regional synthesis—with individual elements remaining exclusive but mutually dependent on the valley environments. It was on these geopolitical and ecological niche that the major spatial pattern in the state emerged. In conventional terms, location of the state has been of crucial importance.

The Brahmaputra valley remained susceptible to frequent waves of migration and invasions. Goalpara and Cachar offered easy access through which the deltaic influences permeated into the region. The mountain passes in the east along the North-Eastern Hills permitted trans-frontier elements to penetrate into the regional space. This called for frequent territorial adjustments between the various groups who were already in occupation of the valley space but also with the new waves of migrants who forced the earlier settlers to either disperse and fragment or move into the interior hills or both. Continuation of these processes brought about distinctly marked areas of attraction and areas of isolation. So that there developed symptoms of differences and disparities within the existing state's territories. Natural endowments and geographical attributes reinforced this. Latter provided each territory and its populace with specific geo-economic considerations. In a way, these encouraged early balkanisation and reflected heterogeneity under more or less similar conditions in the state's landscape. Consequently, with the extension of administration, there emerged contradictions in space arrangements. This was not related to either historical or geographical distinctions. However, such distinctions, proved to be meaningful only in the socio-cultural and politico-economic contexts, if one refuses to accept the existing arrangements.

Geo-political factors have played a crucial role in the evolution and development of the state's political and socio-economic milieu. The balkanisation that had taken place since Independence were largely due to greater impact of social welfare measures and consequent slow rate of economic development. It, then, becomes necessary to understand the basis of these attributes. These constituted the basic features of the pre-colonial, colonial, as well as post-colonial state.

The extent of ancient Assam can be obtained from the Hindu epics and in the Pauranik and Tantric literature; Assam or Pragjyotisha as it was then known, stretched southwards as far as the Bay of Bengal. Its western boundary was the Karatoya. On the other hand, the Puranic literature suggested that Kamrup or Assam embraced almost the entire eastern Bengal, Assam and Bhutan. In the Jogini Tantra, Kamrupa is said to have extended from the Karatoya river on the west to Dikhu on the east and from the mountains of Kanjagiri on the north, to the confluence of the Brahmaputra and the Lakhya river on the south. In other words, it included roughly the present day Brahmaputra valley, Bhutan, Rangpur, Cooch Bihar, the north-east of Mymensingh and, possibly the Garo Hills. Further, this country was divided into four portions, viz., Kampith from the Karatoya to the Sankosh, Ratnapith from the Sankosh to the Rupohi, Suvarnapith from the Rupohi to the Barail and Saumarpith from the Bharali to the Dikrang.

According to Huen Tsang who visited India in the first half of the seventh century A.D., that Kamrupa had a circumference of almost 1,700 miles. Probably, it would have included the whole of Assam, and Bhutan. North Bengal is as far as Karatoya river and the part of Mymensingh, which lies to the east of the old course of the Brahmaputra. Its eastern boundary was line of hills adjacent to the tribes of the Chinese frontier, *i.e.*, it extended as far to the east as did the composite Assam. Buranjis of the Ahoms, provide adequate references to the size and extent of the state between 12th and 18th centuries. Reference about the extent of the boundary of Assam during the Ahom rule is contained in Mir Jumlah's account, who accompanied ShihabbUddin, on his invasion of Assam in 1662. During the Ahom rule, the extent of Assam varied with the change in the leadership.

The Assam valley has been repository of Dravidian, Mongoloid, Austeric and Aryan groups of people. These groups entered the valley at different periods. Initial settlements were temporary. Frequent movements within the valley space coincided with the search for sustainable lands for cultivation with the then available technology and man power. It formed part of the ancient kingdom of Kamrupa. It consisted of numerous tribal kingdoms who were in constant state of dynamic equilibrium with each other. By the Thirteenth Century A.D., the valley was dominated by the Kamata Kingdom, covering the area occupied by the present day districts of Goalpara, Dhubri, Kokrajhar, Bongaigaon, Barpeta, Nalbari, Kamrup, and parts of Morigaon. It lasted upto 1385 A.D. The Bara-Bhuyan Kingdom, covering the area occupied by the present day districts of Darrang, Sonitpur, parts of Lakhimpur, Nagaon, Jorhat and Sibsagar. It lasted upto 1504 A.D. The Kachari Kingdom, covering the area occupied by the present day districts of Nagaon, Jorhat, and Sibsagar. It lasted upto 1536 A.D. The

Chutiya Kingdom of the Bodo-Shan group, covering the area occupied by the present day districts of Dibrugarh, Tinsukia, Lakhimpur and Sibsagar—east of Subansiri and Dihing Rivers. During this period, elements from the Ganga delta and the Tai elements from further east of the region began their periodic forays into the region.

Thus, Assam lay North-East of the province of Bengal. The river Brahmaputra divided the valley into two unequal halves by flowing west to east. Guwahati to Sadiya is about 200 km; its breath, north to south, from the hills of the Garos, Miris, Mishmis, Daflas and Landahs to those Naga tribes is given eight days journey. Its southern mountains touch length-wise the hilly region of Khasia, Kachar and Gonasher and breadth-wise the hills inhabited by the Naga tribes. The land on the north bank of the Brahmaputra is called Uttarkol, and on the southern bank Dakhinkol; Uttarkol stretches from Guwahati to the home of the Miri and Mishmi tribes, and Dakhinkol from the kingdom of the Nak-Kati Rani to the village of Sadiya. Hamilton (1820) stated that Assam adjoined the province of Bengal at the North-Eastern corner, about 91°E longitude, from where it stretches in an easterly direction to an undefined extent; but it is probable that about the 96° east longitude, it meets the northern territory of Ava, and is separated by an intervening space of about 180 miles from the province of Yunan in China.

The Ahoms, comprising essentially of the Tai elements, began their incursions into the valley towards the latter half of the thirteenth century. They were able to bring the upper Brahmaputra valley under their sway. In this initial phase (13th to 16th Century A.D.), they shared the valley with other prominent powers. However, towards the latter half of the sixteenth century, power relationship within the valley were transformed. It coincided with the emergence of the Koch Kingdom covering parts of the present day districts of Goalpara, Dhubri, Kokrajhar, Bongaigaon, Kamrup, Darrang, Sonitpur, and Morigaon. It lasted upto 1587 when it was absorbed by the expanding Ahom kingdom. The Ahom Kingdom enclosed the present day districts of Dibrugarh, Lakhimpur, Tinsukia, and Sibsagar by early fourteenth century. It's westward expansion coincided with the decline and fragmentation of the Kacheri

Koch kingdoms. This empire survived for a long period, *i.e.*, from 1226 to 1826 A.D. By 1587, the Ahoms confronted the Mughals in the west round the Lower Brahmaputra valley, the Burmese along the Patkai ranges in the east and Manipur in the south and south east; while Manipur was also under permanent threat from the east. Initially the Ahoms were successful in subjugating the territories occupied by the Morans, the Borahis, the Naga groups and other inhabitants of the valley. With the decline of the Ahoms, the Singhpos along Patkai range wrested control of the area east of the river Burhi-Dihang in 1794. Following them, the Khamptis established themselves along the river Tengapani and extended their territorial control upto Sadiya.

However, this period also saw the rise of three significant regional powers of the Ahoms, Burma (Kingdom of Ava) and Manipur. These powers between them, controlled the transactions in the region—from the northern and eastern extremity of the Ganga delta through the eastern Hills and plateaux upto the Upper Burma and lower Burma regions. This period also saw inroads made by the Mughals in the west through the Goalpara gateway and through the south-eastern gateway of Cachar from the eastern Ganga delta. The Ahom empire was geopolitically dominated by powerful neighbours whose interests lay in their attempt to fragment the Ahom empire. The Ahoms built strong military-feudal structures adequately reinforced by fort cities, extensive river navigation, strong agrarian economy and a strong feudal bureaucratic military structures. It was largely successful in assimilating many of the elements; thus strengthening plural characteristics. Despite the innovative measures in the structure of control and economy, the Ahom empire succumbed to internal contradictions.

Thus, the ahom empire in the valley extended on both sides of the river Brahmaputra. It was divided into three provinces of Kamrup on the west, Assam proper in the centre, and Sadiya in the eastern extremity. The western province Kamrup, with several subordinate or inter-mixed petty jurisdictions, extended from the British boundary near middle Khamakya (26° 36′N and 92° 56′E), about 130 miles in length, from the boundary, opposite to Goalpara to Nodornbera, a distance of 21 miles, Assam extends for 109 miles. Its width, averages about 30 miles. About 104 miles above Gauhati (91°48′E), the Brahmaputra separates into two branches and encloses an island, five days journey in length and about one in width.

Assam proper, the middle province of the Kingdom is of greater extent than the western. The portion, north of the Brahmaputra was designated as Charidwar, probably exceeds 200 miles in length and 20 in average breadth; but the length on the south side of that river is less considerable. It commences near the middle Kamakhya about 130 miles east, from Goalpara, and reaches to the upper Kamakhya, which is said to be 10 miles below Tikliya Potor Mukh. Within these limits, it comprises of the upper half of the western island formed by Brahmaputra, and includes the island of Majuli, the Brahmaputra and its tributary, the Dihing. Of the third and most remote province nothing is known, except that it is a small side of the Dibrong river, about 95°10′E. The boundary changes that had taken place were mainly restricted to the peripheral region. Ahoms pursued a policy of benevolent neglect as far as the adjacent hilly periphery was concerned. These adjacent hill territories had a weak economic base, and were characterised by difficult and rugged terrain. These along with dense forest cover, acted as a deterrent to accessibility and movement. Physical barrier prevented the core from having any meaningful interaction with its periphery. This enabled these territories to maintain the physical isolation, and reflect multiplicity of ethnic, cultural and regional identities. The Ahom rulers conferred upon these regions, the status of dependencies. They strengthened the economic base of the Brahmaputra valley, which was essentially a rice-based economy.

The eighteenth century saw the gradual decay of the Ahom power, particularly the Ahom control over the region received its first blow from the Moamoria Civil War that took place in 1770, and since then under the impact of the repeated Burmese invasion, which culminated in their occupation of the valley (1817–1824), left the plain a reign of total chaos, lawlessness and oppression. Thus the last of the Ahom ruler had no option but to seek the help of the British, whose rule then extended till the adjoining Bengal plain. It is under such conflicting conditions in Assam, that the British made their appearance.

They forced the Burmese by the Treaty of Yandabo in 1826 to surrender their claim over the region. Thus, according to the Article 2 to the Treaty the Burmese renounced all claims upon and future interference with the principality of Assam and its dependencies, and also with the contiguous petty states of Cachar and Jaintia. This marked the beginning of the new era in the history of Assam and put an end to a glorious rule of the Ahoms and the uninterrupted freedom that the people of Assam enjoyed under them; at the same time the British incorporated the province for the first time within their Indian dominion.

In short, it can be stated that, there is a definite link between political activities and the geographical space. A change in administration or territorial boundary includes a corresponding change in the policy and priorities of development; consequently landscape changes followed. During the Ahom rule, the core of their power, *i.e.*, the Brahmaputra valley, were surrounded practically on all sides by hills, accessible only through the numerous but difficult passes and river routes. The Ahom ruler's policy towards the hilly periphery was essentially that of non-interference, motivated may be by the fact that: possession of extensive unintegrated or economically neglected areas may result in a drain on state resources from the cost of administration and communication construction. Since, their territorial jurisdiction was confined to the long alluvial valley of the Brahmaputra, homogeneous in terms of physiography, economy which was described as a rice economy, and culture, it enabled the Ahoms to administer the region efficiently and effectively in all spheres. Thus the rice economy of the state made considerable progress under their rule. The British interest, on the other hand, was more of economic exploitation, particularly since the discovery of tea and jute in the region. Due to the sporadic raids by the hill tribes, on the valley, it necessitated to exert some measure of control over them, primarily to safeguard their interest and also for reasons of security due to their location in sensitive areas, bordering China and Burma. They, therefore, gradually amalgamated the various political units of the surrounding hill areas. Despite this, their policy was in essence similar to that of their predecessors, *i.e.*, they adopted the policy of conciliation in their dealing with the hill tribes. This policy helped to keep the hill people at bay and at the same time brought about an atmosphere, conducive for their pursuit in the commercial sector of the agricultural economy.

Burmese expansion began in 1750. After consolidation of the immediate environs, Upper Burma proper, they expanded westwards to annex the Arakan coasts. Burma expanded westwards into Manipur and then to the Brahmaputra valley. There were corresponding movements towards the coastal Gangetic delta. These developments found parallels in the Sub-Continent, where the British East India Company was able to seize the political initiative and territorial control to establish an empire. Burmese expansion posed a threat. Though Burma had made frequent armed incursions in Manipur in the past, it was only during the first quarter of the nineteenth century that the decisive phase of Burmese territorial expansion was reached and its implications were abundantly clear. Burma brought Manipur under its sphere of influence and latter was able to effectively dominate the eastern half of the Brahmaputra valley by 1823. Simultaneously, Burma occupied the island of Shahpuri—off the delta coast in the East Bengal, now Bangladesh. Its brief occupation of these areas coincided with decimation of the people of the valley and destruction of the valley economy.

In the meanwhile, the British in India were able to persuade the Jaintia and the Cachar kings for defensive arrangements to meet the increasing Burmese threat in 1824. Subsequently, in 1825, Burmese converged on Cachar. This resulted in the First Anglo-Burmese War. Burma was forced to withdraw from Raha and Kaliabor in the Nagaon sub-region of the valley. This was the western limit of the Burmese expansion in the valley. They were compelled to withdraw from Cachar and Manipur. They capitulated at Rangpur (now in Bangladesh). By the Treaty of Yandabo, 1826, Burma surrendered all its claim over Assam, Manipur, Jaintia, Cachar and Gangetic delta. The British in India subsequently entered into treaty agreements with these powers, but the entire region now lay open to British East India Company's domination and control. As for Assam, particularly the Brahmaputra valley, areas west of Biswanath were incorporated with the Bengal

Province, while areas east of it remained under the nominal control of the Ahoms. These events were followed by the pacification of the Singhpos and Khamptis. It remained the company's responsibility to guarantee internal security.

A portion of Upper Assam, (excluding Muttock and Sadiya) was constituted into a separate principality and was conferred upon the last Ahom King. In 1834, the British of the Brahmaputra valley was divided into four districts, Goalpara, Kamrup, Darrang including Bishwanath and Nagaon Gong. In 1838, due to the incompetence on the last Ahom King, the province under his jurisdiction was annexed and formed the districts of Silpur or Sibsagar, which included the tract south of the old course of Brahmaputra, and Lakhimpur. Again in 1842, Muttock and Sadiya were incorporated into the British territory, and was incorporated to the Lakhimpur district the headquarters of which was transferred to Dibrugarh in the Muttock district. The Colonial territory extended to the districts of Goalpara, Guwahati, Tezpur, Nagaon, Sibsagar and Lakhimpur.

Once the Colonial administration found their footing in the region, it became inevitable for them to be on constant lookout for newer and newer tracts that could be added to their Empire. By 1858, the territorial extent of Assam was bounded on the north-west and north by Burma and the Naga tribes; on the south by Cachar, Manipur, Jaintia and the Khasi hills: and on the west by the British district (Zillah) of Goalpara. It extended from latitude 25° N and from longitude 90°40' to 97°1' E, with an area of 21,805 sq. Miles, and a population at 710,000. Much of the territories that surrounded Assam, *i.e.*, Jaintia, Cachar along with their dependencies, the independent tribal states of the Khasi Hills as well as the other principalities were gradually annexed, on the face of stiff resistance. These were completed within a decade and a half after the Treaty of Yandabo. The first to be incorporated within the administrative set-up was Cachar in 1832, though North Cachar Hills were organised into a separate administrative unit in 1854, after their complete subjection; the Khasi state in 1833, while Jaintia Hills in 1835, and Garo Hills was made into a separate district in 1869, the process to bring them under full control continued till 1873. The Lushais were brought under control during the period 1871–89, and the Lushai Hills was formed into a district in the year 1898. The annexations of Bhutan Duars, the Sadiya, Balipara frontier tracts, the Naga hills etc. were a long process. Only a part of Naga Hills was annexed in 1866, but the control over the Lotha Nagas was possible only in 1878–80 and the Ao Naga as late as 1889. Thus, it was a fact that the boundaries of the British power in North-East India were in fact always moving in a flux, right up to its last days in India. However, Muttock uprising in 1839 compelled the Colonial power to incorporate the entire Upper Brahmaputra valley in 1839. Correspondingly, Cachar sub-region was annexed between 1832 and 1835. Sadiya Tracts were brought under control in 1842. So that all the territories of the Ahom empire were effectively brought under the purview of the British colonial power.

Initially, the Ahom system of administration was adhered to. This was followed by a revenue survey of the valley. This enabled the Colonial administration to assess the resource potentials of the valley and encouraged them to formulate policies that favoured furtherance of their interests in commercial plantations. This was followed by an assessment of land relations. By mid-1830s, the administration promulgated new land policies that were at par with the policies adopted in the rest of the Sub-continent, and ultimately led to the lop sided development of the area (whose impact continued well after Independence). The resultant change had radically transformed the relationships and equations in the valley. It transformed the existing patterns of interactions between various population groups, particularly in their social, cultural, and political transactions. Initially these policies provided little incentives to the inhabitants to participate in the political relations. It is, however, kept them aloof from the economic changes that were gradually introduced in the valley. Spurt in the Colonial economic activities and work of various non-governmental agencies alongwith alphabetisation of the languages and dialects introduced processes that were alien: so that, the state began to exhibit the co-existence of tradition and modernism at the same time. These changes coincided with the large scale movement of population from the Ganga delta and the Chotanagpur sub-regions of the sub-continent who moved into the region as a response to demand for manpower required by administration and commercial activities. These introduced complexity in a difficult scenario.

Be that as it may, administratively the state was initially included in the Province of Bengal: the Bengal Presidency under a non-regulatory system. In 1874, it was declared as Scheduled District. It was separated from the Bengal Province to form a Chief Commissioner's Province. It consisted of the districts of Goalpara, Garo Hills, Kamrup, Khasi Hills, Jaintia Hills, Darrang, Nagaon, Lakhimpur and Sibsagar (1875). In 1905, as a result of Curzon's plan for the Partition of Bengal, it was included in the province of East Bengal and Assam. However, with the annulment of the Partition Plan in 1911–12, it was re-designated as the Chief Commissioner's Province. In 1921, it was elevated to a Governors' Province. It, then, consisted of the districts of (a) Goalpara (originally part of the Bengal province), Kamrup, Darrang, Lakhimpur and Nagaon in the Brahmaputra valley; (b) The Barak-Surma Valley comprising the areas of Sylhet (now in Bangla desh) and Cachar; and (c) the hill areas of Garo, Khasi, Jaintia, Naga and Lushai areas along with the areas of Mikir and Barail ranges; administratively, areas of the North-Eastern Frontier Tracts (now Arunachal Pradesh) were brought under the purview of State's Governor.

Independence had brought about a tremendous change in the existing politico-administrative landscape. Partition resulted in the loss of territory whereby the state lost most of its jute producing areas to Pakistan (Bangladesh). Influx of a sizeable number of refugees and dislocation created due to snapping off, of railways, road and water communication with the rest of the country made the situation of the state quite difficult. In addition, the state extended administration to the hill areas. This in a way encouraged the growing feeling of alienation amongst the hill people. Consequently, there began to demand autonomy for their respective territories. This eventually led to administrative re-organisation.

The state of Assam in the post-1947 phase was territorially defined as being located in the North-East border of India and is surrounded on all sides by the other independent states like Bhutan and Tibet (China) in the north-west and East Pakistan (now Bangladesh) on the west. It was surrounded by mountainous ranges at least on three sides, on the north is the Himalaya shutting off the tablelands of Bhutan and Tibet; on the North-East is the Patkai range along with a series of other hills which merge with those forming the limits of the independent republic of Burma and part 'C' state of Tripura. It is only on the west where it adjoins West Bengal and Eastern Pakistan that there are no hills. It comprises the whole of the valley of Brahmaputra down to the point where the river emerging on the Bengal delta takes a sudden southwards curve and a portion of the valley of Surma together with the intervening range of hills which forms the watershed between them.

At the time of Partition and Independence in 1947, the Province of Assam minus the district of Sylhet (a referendum was held in Sylhet to decide whether the area was to go to India or Pakistan; it went in favour of Pakistan), an amendment was made to the Assam land revenue regulation in 1947. This amendment re-defined 33 tribal blocks and belts (10 tribal belts and 23 tribal blocks). Subsequently based on this, there were two in the then district of Goalpara, 8 each in Kamrup and Darrang, three in North Lakhimpur and 12 in Nagaon districts. In 1954, Tuensang Frontier Division of the North-Eastern Frontier Tract (re-named as the North-Eastern Frontier Area) was transferred to Assam and became a combined district of the Naga Hills and Tuensang Area.

The post Independence period witnessed a significant change in the relationship between the hills and the Assam valley. Independence led the government to totally abandon the policy of non-interference in the hill regions, due to their strategic location along the borders with China, East Pakistan (now Bangladesh) and Myanmar. Thus, there were concerted efforts on the part of the state to bring these regions within the mainstream of the country. This resulted in bringing about a growing feeling of alienation among the Hill Units of Assam. In this context, it is fair to state that dissidents normally occurred amongst sections of the population who regarded themselves as being distinctive in language, religion and origin.

Distinct ethnic, linguistic and cultural identity of the hill areas fostered the desire to separate from the composite state of Assam, to form an autonomous state of their own. Due to their location in a sensitive and strategic region, it was not possible for the state to ignore the aspirations of the people. This ultimately resulted in re-organisation that left Assam, a shadow of her former self. In the process, the first to break away from the threshold of Assam were the inhabitants of the Naga Hills and the Tuensang Frontier Division, which was separated from Assam, to form the state of Nagaland in December, 1963 (it consisted of the entire district of the former Naga Hills of Assam and part of Tuensang, part of NEFA). This served as a catalyst for the other hill tribal areas of Assam to seek their own state. Meghalaya, Mizoram, and Arunachal Pradesh were separated from Assam almost around the same time. Initially, Meghalaya was conferred the status of Autonomous state within the state of Assam on 2nd April, 1970, it became a full-fledged state on January 21st, 1972, comprising of Khasi, Jaintia and Garo hills with an area of 22,500 sq. km. Since then there had been no changes in the external boundaries of the state.

Mizoram as a Union Territory was separated from Assam on 21st January, 1972, covering the erstwhile Mizo Hills district of Assam, with an area of 21,087 sq. km. The other area was North-East Frontier Agency. In 1972, under the provisions of the North-East Frontier Areas (Re-Organisation) Act (1971) NEFA was declared as a Union Territory and came to be known as Arunachal Pradesh. It became a state in 1987.

The repercussions of all these activities had left a marked impression in the economy of the state of Assam. This may partly account for the slow progress made by the economy particularly agriculture in spite of decades of planned development. From the development administrative point of view, the state has undergone series of changes, from nearly 6 districts in the late 1940s to 10 in the 1970s to 23 in mid-1990s. Today, in 1996, the state of Assam has 23 districts, 45 sub-divisions, 134 Revenue Circles and 131 Community Development Blocks, besides having scores of Panchayats and Anchalik Samities. Table 1 gives the necessary details.

On the basis of the above table, one can infer that:

Table 1: Administrative Divisions—Assam—1995

Districts	Area in sq. km	Sub-Divisions	Revenue Circles	C.D. Blocks
Dhubri	2838.0	3	8	7
Kokrajhar	3498.0	2	5	5
Bongaigaon	2159.0	3	4	5
Goalpara	1910.8	1	5	4
Barpeta	3245.0	2	8	8
Nalbari	2257.0	1	9	7
Kamrup	4345.0	3	14	11
Darrang	4810.0	2	9	6
Sonitpur	5324.0	2	7	7
Lakhimpur	2277.0	2	6	6
Dhemaji	3237.0	2	4	3
Morigaon	1559.2	1	5	4
Nagaon	3973.0	3	9	10
Golaghat	3502.0	2	5	6
Jorhat	2851.0	2	5	6
Sibsagar	2668.0	2	6	6
Dibrugarh	3381.0	1	7	6
Tinsukia	3790.0	3	4	4
Karbi Anglong	10434.0	3	—	10
NC Hills	4888.0	2	—	4
Karimganj	1829.0	1	5	5
Hailakandi	1327.0	1	4	3
Cachar	3786.0	1	5	7

- That 18 plain districts of the state, located largely in the Brahmaputra valley, enclose 71.62 percent or 56,174 sq. km. of the state,
- that the districts of Karbi Anglong and North Cachar Hills, occupying 19.53 percent or 15,322 sq. km., form the Hill and Plateau section of the state; and,
- that the districts of Karimganj, Hailakandi and Cachar occupying 6922 sq. km. or 8.8 percent of the state area, form the Barak valley sub-division of the state.

Within this truncated state itself, the re-organisation of districts—from 5 in 1950s to 10 in 1970s and to 23 in 1990s. Further, because of uneven and lop sided development, inadequate infrastructure facilities and others, several population sub-groups are presently pressing for separate autonomous administrative status. This has brought the spectre of possible re-organisation.

Causes of Rapid Growth of Population

The rapid growth of population in Assam has been due to the following factors *i.e.*, (a) natural increase, (b) immigration from Bangladesh and Nepal and (c) immigration from other states. The difference between the birth rate and the death rate of population in Assam has been consistently high. The birth rate was 46.7 per thousand of population during 1941–51. It increased to 49.3 per thousand during the 1951–61 decade. But the rate came down to 38.5 per thousand during 1961–71. Up to 1925, the death rate in Assam was very high due to epidemics like Kala Azar, cholera, malaria. But it gradually went down. During the 1941–51 decade, the death rate was 31.8 per thousand. During 1971–79, the birth rate came down from 38.5 to 31.0 per thousand population. The death rate, on the hand, went down from 17.8 to 11.3 per thousand population during the same period. Both economic and non-economic factors are responsible for high birth rate. Poverty, illiteracy, religious and social belief, low standard of living high infant mortality, universality of marriage etc., are other factors that have been responsible for this. High illiteracy rate, particularly among women is common, though there has been a marginal improvement in recent years. The death rate has declined due to improvement in medical facilities, control of epidemics, improvements in economic conditions etc.

Density of Population

The density of population of Assam in 1991 was 284 persons per sq. km. as against all India average of 265 persons per sq. km. In fact, Assam had more persons per sq. km. than the national average in 1971 and 1981. Density of population in Assam increased by about 36 percent during 1971–81 compared to 33 percent in the country. Table 2 provides for the variations in the density pattern in Assam and national average between 1901 and 1991. The increase in the density during this period has significantly led to reduction in the man-land ratio among others, in the state. Besides, within the state, there is a marked variation in the density.

Table 2: Decadal Variation of Population 1901–11 to 1981–91

in percentages

	1901–11	1911–21	1921–31	1931–41	1941–51	1951–61	1961–71	1971–81	1981–91
T	16.99	20.48	19.91	20.40	19.93	34.98	34.95	23.36	24.26
R	16.91	20.08	19.70	20.16	18.46	30.87	32.62	21.92	22.56
U	20.55	36.80	27.58	28.30	65.35	26.57	65.01	38.25	39.58

Source: Census of India, 1991.

Rural-Urban Differences

Population in the state is predominantly rural in character. In 1951, 95.35 percent of the total population of the state was rural: of which rural settlements with a population of 2000 accounted for 50 percent of total rural population: followed by 42 percent of the rural population in villages less than 2000 population and remaining in villages more than 2000 population. In 1961 rural population accounted for 92.5 percent of the total population. In 1991, Dhemaji and Nalbari districts of the state had the highest percentage share of rural population. These districts were followed by Darrang, Marigaon, Golaghat, Sibsagar, Karimganj, Barpeta, Goalpara, Sonitpur, Lakhimpur, Bongaigaon, and Cachar. Rest of the districts had percentage rural population below 90 percent but above 65 percent of the total population.

The percentage of people living in the rural areas in Assam was 91 percent in 1971 as compared to 80.09 percent in the country. In other words, urbanisation has been slow if not stagnant in Assam. The proportion of rural population in the country declined to 76.37 percent in 1981 (as no Census was possible in the state in 1981). The urban population accounted for 10.29 percent of the total population of the state. According to the 1991 Census, the rural population of the state was 88.92 percent as against 74.28 percent in the country.

One can clearly infer from the available Census records and the works of Mills and Hamilton that the population of the state after the Treaty of Yandabo, 1826. The due impetus was given through the establishment of tea and associated ancillary industries with the British capital. From Table 3 it may be observed that the growth of population in Assam has been very rapid. During the period 1901–1981 the population

Table 3: Decadal Variations in Population—Assam, 1901–1991

(in percentage)

Districts	1901–11	1911–21	1921–31	1931–41	1941–51	1951–61	1961–71	1971–91
Dhubri	33.76	11.42	6.05	10.57	15.21	27.62	40.51	56.57
Kokrajhar	16.70	90.75	39.68	26.59	0.50	-46.34	54.30	76.73
Bongai-gaon	29.94	26.94	15.94	20.85	4.00	-60.51	40.19	64.64
Goalpara	27.41	37.07	20.50	7.73	11.33	37.22	45.88	54.12
Barpeta	00.02	34.04	69.02	44.06	18.77	32.62	35.48	43.02
Nalbari	13.33	14.20	27.92	29.28	9.48	49.62	42.02	49.27
Kamrup	11.16	7.06	9.32	14.60	21.87	37.73	38.80	65.72
Darrang	-0.25	11.78	26.00	35.30	24.13	44.75	43.24	55.63
Sonitpur	24.33	40.69	20.50	19.73	24.26	35.82	27.62	57.14
Lakhim-pur	17.30	22.82	25.99	36.98	21.62	50.46	43.39	56.29
Dhemaji	45.30	63.30	16.90	8.41	-3.35	68.56	103.42	107.50
Morigaon	15.50	31.99	41.66	30.87	23.32	37.89	37.51	50.90
Nagaon	15.80	31.94	41.35	10.34	11.41	35.91	38.99	51.26
Golaghat	16.25	20.14	18.29	1.40	19.52	26.04	30.85	58.12
Jorhat	16.32	17.34	8.88	15.12	15.03	15.03	15.03	24.17
Sibsagar	13.41	20.46	14.44	15.64	15.98	23.36	19.47	38.76
Dibru-garh	27.10	38.40	22.34	10.87	26.23	31.35	22.93	37.78
Tinsukia	21.10	28.32	27.00	34.77	11.09	35.92	31.02	33.12
Karbi Anglong	NA	NA	NA	NA	30.96	79.21	68.28	74.72
NC Hills	47.03	5.92	13.60	13.75	6.16	36.95	40.00	98.30
Karim ganj	12.94	3.19	5.91	9.52	29.87	27.96	25.13	142.03
Haila-kandi	16.09	7.59	7.09	10.20	17.48	27.23	23.61	45.94
Cachar	12.33	5.93	7.60	13.00	19.93	34.99	23.92	22.60
ASSAM	16.99	20.48	19.91	20.40	23.96	47.59	34.95	53.26

Source: Census of India, 1991.

in Assam increased by 504.83 percent as against 187.05 percent in the country. The decadal variation in Assam during the period 1911–1951 was on an average 19.4 percent. In the subsequent decades from 1951–1971, the percentage increase in population was 34.97. As the state did not have Census in 1981, the projected growth rate of population in Assam during 1971–1981 was 36.05 percent as against the country's population growth at 25.0 percent. Among all the states, the highest increase in population between 1901–1981 was in Assam. The subsequent Census 1981–91 saw the growth rate at 26.63 percent which was much higher than the national average. Significantly, this growth rate of 53.26 percent for the period 1971–91 for Assam after the re-organisation of the states in the North-East India. It is estimated that Assam will have 305 lakh population by March 2001, registering cumulative annual growth rate of 2.2 percent between 1981 and 2001 against 1.8 percent for the country in the same period.

Growth trend of population in the state, is not uniform. In the Karbi Anglong and N.C. Hills districts (First Census started in 1951), the growth rate was high. During 1951–1971, the growth of population in these two districts was 62.79 percent and 74.72 percent, as against the state's growth rate of 34.95 percent and 26.63 percent in the same period. In Goalpara district, it was 44.22 percent and 54.12 percent, which was higher than that in any other plain districts of Assam. However, the highest growth rate was in the district of Kokrajhar with 76.78 percent for the 1971–91 period with Sibsagar district having the lowest growth rate of 16.55 percent in 1971–91 period.

In other words, in 1901, Assam had 3.29 million persons, as against 238.4 million persons in the country. In 1991, the total population of Assam went up to 22.30 million as against 844.32 million in the country. The percentage variation of population between 1901 and 1991 in Assam was 577.7 percent as against 254.2 percent in the country. The percentage variation of population in Assam and India between 1901 and 1981 was 504.83 percent and 187.05 percent respectively. The growth of population in Assam during the 1981–91 decade was 23.63 percent as against all India average of 23.50 percent.

Schedule Caste and Schedule Tribe Population

There are 16 scheduled castes and 23 scheduled tribes consisting 6.24 percent and 10.99 percent respectively of the total population of the state. The Namasudras and Kaibartas are the major scheduled casts. The major tribes are the Bodos (6.1 million), Kacharis including Sonowals (0.2 million) and Dimasas (0.04 million). According to the 1991 Census, total Scheduled Caste population in the state was 1,659,412 persons (of which 1,430,131 were males); the total Scheduled

Tribes population was 2,574,441 persons (of which 1,777,308 were males).

In other words, 1991 Census identified 7.26 percent and 13.32 percent of the total population of the state as to belong to the Schedule Caste and schedule Tribes categories. Nagaon with 11.43percent and N.C. Hills with 0.24 percent had the highest and lowest population of Schedule Caste population in the state. While Kokrajhar with 11.46 percent and Cachar with 0.02 percent had the highest and lowest schedule Tribe populations in the state.

Age Structure and Sex Ratio

The age structure determines the proportion of the labour force in the total population. The age structure is often studied by classifying the population into dependent children (below 15 years), economically active population (between 15–59 years) and aged dependants (60 years and above). The population in the age group of 15–59 can contribute to productive efforts of the community. According to the 1971 census, the proportion of dependent children was 46.95 percent and economically active population was 48.34 percent. The proportion of child population was higher than the all India average of 42 percent. In other words, Assam's population is characterised by the predominance of young people.

Occupational Structure

Like any developing economy, the occupational structure in Assam is more tilted towards agricultural and agro-allied activities. In the 1991 Census, divided into the population into two categories, viz., workers and non-workers, and placed them as belonging to workers of economic activity, viz., Primary sector, Secondary sector and Tertiary sector. The primary sector comprises of the industrial categories from 1 to 3, the secondary sector of 4 and 5 and the tertiary sector of 6 to 9. The percentage of population in the primary, secondary and tertiary sectors was 76.69, 4.50 and 18.81 respectively. In Assam 76.69 percentage of population was dependent on agriculture and allied activities against 72.05 percent in the country. Even within the region, Manipur has only 71.28 percent population dependent on the primary sector. In the 1991 census, population was classified into total population, Main workers and marginal workers. The main workers were again divided into (a) cultivator, (b) agricultural labourers, (c) household industry, manufacturing, processing, servicing and repairs; and (d) other workers. As per this economic classification, the percentage of main workers to the total population in Table 4.

47.55 percent of the total population of the state is main workers and 2.77 percent is the marginal workers. Out of the main workers, 51.20 percent is the cultivators, 12.72 percent is agricultural labourers, 1.91 percent workers are engaged in household industry, manufacturing, processing, servicing and repair, and 34.18 percent is the other workers. The percentage of cultivators and agricultural labourer together is 63.92.

Literacy

The literacy rate in Assam was 27.9 percent in 1961. It increased to 28.1 percent in 1971. This rate in literacy in Assam is not significant when compared to rise in all India literacy

Table 4: Composition of Workers—Assam, 1991

Kamrup	613340	398674	581362	361768	32038	25906
Darrang	59748	539579	420891	396692	138857	138087
Sonitpur	614362	582223	490532	458567	124030	123656
Lakhimpur	353090	337733	265394	250472	87696	87261
Dhemaji	214816	270037	177629	174115	37187	35922
Morigaon	210022	198493	187673	176521	22349	21972
Nagaon	641133	582640	564911	508140	76222	74500
Golaghat	327254	310646	287415	271445	39839	39201
Jorhat	306852	263795	279732	237679	27120	25616
Sibsagar	371061	319617	331402	310421	39659	38196
Dibrugarh	413315	357467	370877	316727	42438	40740
Tinsukia	396073	343317	355062	304615	41011	38702
Karbi Anglong	280786	257878	250521	236600	22210	21278
N.C. Hills	56791	46197	55754	45484	1097	713
Karimganj	247086	230158	222708	206234	24378	23924
Hailakandi	180876	150844	128499	119346	32427	31698
Cachar	437283	402324	350989	317224	86294	85090
ASSAM	8108785	7334414	7068363	6316357	1040422	1018057

Source: Census of India, 1991.

rate from 24.0 percent in 1961 to 29.5 percent in 1971 and 53.42 percent in 1971–81 period. The important feature of the literacy rate is the considerable improvement in female literacy. The female literacy increased from 15.1 percent in 1961 to 18.6 percent in 1971 to 339.42 percent in 1971–91 period. The corresponding figure for male literacy was 37.3 percent in 1961, which went down to 36.7 percent in 1971 to 63.86 percent in 1971–91 period. Sibsagar had the highest percentage of literacy (36.6%) and Karbi Anglong the lowest percent (19.2) in the state. In terms of literacy Assam ranks twelfth in the country.

Language

Retracing earlier arguments in this section, it can be said that the language diversity both at broader state level and specifically at micro-level had resulted in ethnic consciousness. Consequent efforts have been directed towards sustained linguistic and/or ethnic identification. The resultant ethnic fragmentation at all levels carried with it the potential for conflict that has been, in cases, turned into an actuality. The population in the state can be classified on the basis of their degree of ethnic heterogeneity. There are two major groups of languages in the state, Assamese and Bengali. In addition, there are eight more languages that are spoken by more than one percent each of the population of the state.

Agriculture

The state of agriculture, at the time of British annexation of the region, has been aptly described by Mills (1853). It was part of the overall assessment of resources and possibilities of their exploitation. These assessments considered the valley to be singularly preoccupied with agriculture; improvements in agriculture was the only means through which resources could be effectively channelled, ameliorate the conditions of the people, advance manufactures and commerce etc. The soils of Assam is favourable for the productions both of the tropical and temperate regions. Silk, cotton, tea and variety of other valuable, products grew luxuriantly and it required only the introduction of an improved method of agriculture to render the produce ten-fold more. The implements used for agricultural purpose were primitive and of simplest kind. The people were ignorant of the growth of a variety of produce of commerce which, would even without the aid of human labour grow spontaneously in the forest of Assam. The means of irrigation and drainage were seldom resorted to. Generally no attempts were made to create embankments, or devise means for the protection of the lands from the encroachments of floods and other accidents.

The consequence is drought or inundation often entirely destroyed the crops. It also reduced the population to wretchedness and misery. The crude state of agriculture prevented the farmers raising more than one crop throughout the year. It was evident that there was ample scope, where intervention on the part of the Colonial Government might have encouraged development of traditional agriculture on modern lines. However, the overriding concern of the British was to establish a commercial agricultural economy, from where they would derive maximum economic benefits. With the discovery of suitable adaptation of tea cultivation in areas that were partially suitable for rice cultivation in the state, an altogether a different approach was adopted towards the then existing agriculture. The Colonial objective of maximisation of economic gain and to feed the manufacturing industries in England. The British policies towards agricultural development were entirely limited to tea and such crops where the expected dividends were the highest; therefore, the growth of the tea plantations, commercialisation of such crops as jute, tobacco, opium, diversification of agriculture, received special impetus. Consequent upon such policies, the acreage and production of cash crops increased several folds. The spectacular growth of Tea Plantation and increase in jute cultivation, became the landmark. Owing to shortages of local labour these activities were largely carried out through immigrant labour.

It could be ascertained from the available literature that out of the total cropped area in 1901, rice cultivation which occupied 71 percent, this subsequently increased marginally to 72 percent, an absolute increase of 2.3 times. The area under rape and mustard seeds registered a significant increase, from

0.16 million acres in 1901 to 0.29 million acres in 1946. The area under tea cultivation showed a gradual increase till 1936–37 and remained stagnant till 1947. This was largely attributed to the fact that tea cultivation was dependent on international markets and was a highly organised industry requiring specialised skill that did not allow the internal economic forces to affect its growth. On the other hand, during the first half of the twentieth century, there was a remarkable increase in the acreage under jute from 5000 acres in 1901 to 0.29 million acres in 1939–40. Jute came to be treated as a commercial cash crop. This enabled the Colonial power to dominate the global trade. However, area under jute declined to 0.18 million acres in 1946–47.

Assam is predominantly an agricultural state with major emphasis on Kharif food grains production. Around 65 percent of the labour force is engaged in this sector. The average per capita food grains production in Assam during the triennial ended 1990–91 was 135 kg, as against all India average of 205 kg. Assam is deficient in food grains. Among food grains, rice is the only major crop grown in the state. Of the total food grains production in the state, rice alone accounted for 94 percent. But the average per hectare production of rice in Assam is much below the all India average. The area under rice cultivation in 1980–81 was 2275 hectares. In 1990–91, it has gone up to 2491 ha, showing an increase of 9.5 percent area under rice cultivation. The compound annual rate of increase between the triennial ended 1980–81 and 1990–91 was 0.8 percent. Though the total area under food grains has increased from 2558.1 ha in 1986–87 to 2719 ha in 1990–91, there has been fall in the area under wheat, grain tur and other pulses, and mustard, jute and mesta and sugar cane during 1986–87 to 1990–91. There has been some increase in the area under potatoes and bananas.

These developments exerted their cost in the form of neglect of the traditional sector. The mode of production in the traditional sector continued to be dominated by traditional crops and seeds, outmoded techniques, while the use of fertiliser or irrigation remained practically non-existent. Thus agricultural development was uneven, while the Colonial power devoted their efforts towards the expansion and development of the plantation sector.

Agriculture contributes more than 50 percent of the State Domestic Product (SDP). The share of agriculture was 57.6 percent in the total SDP in Assam in 1970–71 at current prices. This has declined to 42.6 percent in 1984–85 at current prices and 48 percent at 1970–71 prices. In 1985–86, its share was 50.7 percent and 50.4 percent in 1990–91 at 1970–71 prices. This suggested an essentially agrarian character of the economy and as a consequence the underdeveloped character of Assam's economy. There has not been any significant increase in the gross sown area in the state since 1947. Neither was it proportionate to the growth of the population nor was it adequate to meet the requirements of industrial development of the state. As a result, the state became a net importer of the food grains. Besides, (i) rapid increase in and growth of the size of labour force; (ii) increasing pressure on land; and, (iii) increasing demand for raw materials to sustain developmental activities, relentlessly put pressure on agriculture. Yet, Assam contributed about 50 percent of the total tea production in the country. Its share in the foreign exchange earnings from this head is about 60 percent. Jute is another important commercial crop that contributed substantially to the revenue of the state. In spite of this, agriculture continues to stagnate.

Cropping Pattern

Growth in agriculture is largely determined by the area available for cultivation. This is limited by the availability of land extended through reclamation (and to an extent from deforestation. It is to be noted that the state is covered by hills, rivers, beels, and other low lying water logged area and sandy riverine islands making the extension of cultivation difficult). However, the land use changes have played moderating role. Temporal changes in the cropping patterns are reflected by changing land use pattern.

By turn of the present century, 90 percent of the total cultivated land of the then Assam province, was under food grains with the remaining area under non-food grain crops. This situation drastically changed with the Partition and

Independence; so that by 1958–59, area under food grain crops declined to 84 percent. Of the area under food grains, rice occupied 64.8 percent, and was followed by tea with 6.2 percent, rape and mustard with 5 percent, jute with 3.7 percent, sugar cane with 1 percent and other crops with 19 percent. By 1980–81, area under food grains declined to approximately 82 percent with rice occupying an area of 75.9 percent, wheat with 3.4 percent, pulses with 3.8 percent and total non-food grain crops with 15.8 percent of the area under cultivation. This situation in 1990–91 was approximately placed at 80 percent, with rice occupying an area of 76 percent, wheat with 2.5 percent, pulses with 3.4 percent and total non-food grain crops with 16.5 percent. However, by 1994–95, area under food grains was about 83 percent with rice at 76.1 percent, wheat with 2.5 percent, pulses with 3.2 percent and non-foodgrains with 16.5 percent of the area available for cultivation. Correspondingly, during this period, total food grain production rose from 1.7 MT in 1960–61 to 2.3 MT in 1970–71, to 2.7 MT in 1980–81, to 3.44 MT in 1990-91, to 3.53 MT in 1993–94 and to 3.49 MT in 1994-95. This increase has been partially due to the introduction of HYV of seeds in the Brahmaputra and Barak valleys. In particular, area under HYV of paddy increased from 0.29 Mha in 1975–76 to 1.15 Mha in 1993–94. Following tables indicate the trend in the cropping pattern from I980–81 to 1992–93 in the state. They suggest that during this period, the rate of growth has been slow in area, production and productivity of five major food grain crops in the State.

The total cropped area of the state was 2.8 Mha in 1970–71. This has increased to 3.8 Mha in 1985–86 (constituting 42% of the total geographical area of the state). This is against the all India figure of 50 percent cropped area. Of the total cropped area, 75 percent area is under food crops and 25 percent under non-food crops. Rice, maize, wheat, small millets and other cereals are important cereal crops. Gram, tur, and other pulses are under pulses, rape and mustard, linseed and castor are in oil seed category. Besides, there are sugar cane and potato. Other important crops are tobacco, sweet potato, and chillies.

Causes of Low Productivity

There are a number of factors, which are responsible for the low productivity of agriculture in Assam. They can be grouped under general, institutional, and natural factors. General factors are mainly the social environment and the pressure of population. These can be identified as

a) Social Environment
b) Population Pressure
c) Institutional Factors

i) Land Tenure System
ii) Size of Land Holding
iii) Share Cropping
iv) Credit Facilities
v) Technological Factors
vi) Livestock and Animal Husbandry

Assam has a large livestock population but the quality is very poor. The cattle in the State are small in size. The number of cattle per acre of cultivated area is highest in Assam of all states in India. The contribution of State income from the animal husbandry sector is only 4 percent as against 7 percent for all India. The number of livestock and poultry and their products in the State are shown below State and Agriculture.

During the last more than four decades, there has been an expansion in the Department and also in its activities. These include agricultural education, research and extension. The Assam Agricultural College was set up in 1948. In 1969, the Assam Agricultural University was set up. Besides, a number of Gram Sevak Training Centres at Kahikuchi (Guwahati), Arunachal (Silchar) and Jorhat, a Krishi Vikas at Tezpur, the Gossaigoan Kishan Vidyapith, the second Agricultural College was set up at Biswanath Chariali in 1986–87. In the field of agricultural extension a number of agricultural extension programs beginning under the National Extension Service and Community Development Program have been taken up. Since April, 1985, the National Agricultural Extension Project III has been introduced. Besides, a number of ancillary institutions have been developed, viz., Assam Seed Corporation, (1969), Assam Agro-Industries Development Corporation (1967),

Assam State Seed Agency (1985), Assam State Agricultural Produce Marketing Board (1977–78), Assam State Minor Irrigation Development Corporation, Assam Plantation Crop Development Corporation and the Agricultural Farming Corporation (1970). Distribution of agricultural inputs is being done by the Department of Agriculture, Assam Seed Corporation and the Assam Agro-Industries Development Corporation Besides, the STATFED has also been introduced in distribution of seeds, fertilisers etc. The Department of Agriculture introduced the high Yielding Variety of paddy in the state in 1965–66. A special rice production program was introduced in 1985–86. Project Assistance of Small and Marginal Farmers for agricultural production and the National Oil Seed Development Project etc., are being implemented by the Department. The Department has also set up 58 Agro Service Centres in the state.

Recent Development

Agriculture is the main stay of the state's economy. However, it suffers from a number of inhibiting factors. The method of cultivation is still traditional and in the hill areas, shifting cultivation continues. Productivity of agriculture is one of the lowest in the country. The use of fertilisers and consumption of electricity are very low. Mechanisation have not been carried on due to many and varied factors. The flood problem continues to create havoc to agriculture. Irrigation facilities have not developed to provide regular and assured water supply for agriculture. In order to develop agriculture, these factors have to be tackled properly. The flood problem calls for a long-term solution. Likewise there is a need for curbing fragmentation and sub-division of holdings by taking suitable measures, so that mechanisation can be introduced. The use of improved inputs, manures, fertilisers, seeds, etc., depends upon the farmer's education. There is always a resistance to new things. The resistance can be overcome by persuasion, education and motivation of the farmers. In this respect the agricultural extension agents have a big role to play. All these will help in the development of agriculture in the state.

Assam is rich in raw materials. These can be advantageously used for encouraging industrial development. As of today, it's industrial economy is unintegrated. Resources remain under utilised. In fact, industrial development of the state is handicapped by its isolation from the rest of the country, inadequate infrastructure and a small local market. The traditional cottage industries employ, outdated and cost intensive technology. These are compounded by insufficient capital and lack of skilled labour. There are less than 100 persons per lakh of population, supported by industrial activities in every thousand square kilometer area of the state. The state has, on an average, only 2 percent of India's total registered factories in comparison to 22 percent in West Bengal and 16 percent in Maharashtra in the period 1960 to 1990.

Assam received strong stimuli from the plantation sector for the development of tea, coal, petroleum and ancillary industrial units from 1850s onwards. Since then only oil and tea industries have made significant advances. The present position of the state's industrial economy is conspicuous by notable absence of specialised units operating with the latest processes and technology. These are interspersed with the declining traditional cottage industries employing antiquated methods and techniques of production. No commensurate development of industries with diversified economic-production base has taken place to fill the gap. Though initial efforts in planned development saw emergence of public and private sector, their contribution has been in fits and starts. This effort was seriously handicapped by events of 1962, 1965 and early 1980s (this coupled with natural calamities like annual recurring floods, etc., inhibited the industrial development). Since then, socio-political developments , such as administrative re-organisations, problems of the immigrants have in more than one way contributed in retarding the industrial/economic development of the state. Thus, considering the potential of resources—human, agriculture and natural resources, for industrial development of the state only a fraction of the potential has been exploited so far. Except for tea and oil and associated ancillary and secondary servicing units, industrial activity in the true sense of the term in Assam has not taken off properly. The efforts to develop the down stream industries with Bongaigaon as the core and the establishment of industrial estates in the various districts, are initiatives in this direction.

Floods

Floods have occurred regularly in this century. According to data available from the Central Water Commission (CWC) from 1953 to 1984, an average of 0.8 Mha were affected by floods annually. The maximum area affected was 3.15 Mha in 1954. The maximum population affected was 5.68 million in 1984. The maximum damage in a year Rs. 561.8 million occurred in 1983 whereas the average annual damage was approximately Rs. 139 million. These are suggestive of the fact that the incidence of floods are increasing. The existing trend also indicates that the area affected by floods during the 1980s was higher than in any of the previous decades for which data is available. The 1988 flood affected 4.22 Mha well over the maximum of 3.15 Mha in 1954. The largest number of people ever affected was also in 1988, 12.68 million. The number of people affected per hectare of flood affected area and the amount of damages per hectare of flood affected area have been rising steadily. This has undermined the efforts that were directed to improve agriculture.

Flood situation in the state from 1987 onwards began to come in several waves. The annual feature was characterised by the first wave sometimes in the month of May that swamped on an about 16 districts affecting 1.5 million people. The second in June affected 2.4 million people spread over 17 districts. A third wave affected four districts in July. The fourth in August, the most severe swamped 17 districts. A total of 3.82 Mha and 8.41 million people were affected by the fourth wave alone. Some districts like Nagaon and parts of Karbi Anglong even experienced a fifth wave. The damage to crops, from 1987 onwards averaged Rs. 3340 million annually. This was besides the damages caused to property, human lives and disruption of transport linkages and networks. Besides, the scale and intensity of floods in normal years, affected about 2,000 villages in the state. But from 1987 onwards this increased to 7,290 and in 1988, it was 8,770. And, when one considers the Census figures of the total number of villages in Assam at

21,995, nearly 40 percent of the total villages were subjected to the impact of the floods from 1987 onwards.

Population of the state, particularly in the Brahmaputra Barak plains has been growing rapidly. This has shown an increase from 3.29 million in 1901 to 22.29 million in 1991. This rapid growth encouraged encroachment of riverine areas. As a result, natural backwaters have been constricted. Along with other factors, these have increased sedimentation. In normal circumstances, abandoned channels and horseshoe lakes absorbed the initial impact of floods. Their reclamation for human occupancy have led to far reaching impact on flood management in the state. This has increased the frequency of floods and that too with greater intensity; thereby, some 253 villages and 8,091 hectares of land in Assam were annually affected by erosion by the Brahmaputra.

Reclamation of the spill over areas, *i.e.*, of bils and other natural backwaters, had disastrous impact on the agricultural profile of the state. Several of these natural spillways existed in Lakhimpur, Nagaon, Kamrup an Goalpara. Their ecological role in maintaining the balance favourable for continuous agricultural activity is only now being appreciated. The fact that the bils and depressions predominate the flood plains is an indication of their role in maintaining the hydrological balance of the river. Besides, pronounced Jhum cultivation in the hill sections devastated vast areas south of the Brahmaputra. Its' consequence (the northern tributaries of the Brahmaputra which bring more silt and floods), is now attributed as one of the encouraging factors for increasing incidence of floods in the plains.

In view of these developments, scholars have initiated studies to identify alternative land use patterns. This included the need to evolve a strategy to modify the cropping system in such a way as to overcome the impact of floods. The initial generalisations indicated the need for restructuring the cropping pattern to cope with floods. Except for chronically affected areas, all areas can be brought under appropriate land use. The high flood season coincides with main crop of Assam the *Sali* paddy from June to November. Usually 75 percent of the flood damage is to crops. The *Sali* crop occupies more than 75 percent of the total cropped area. While early floods in the first week of June destroy the standing *Ahu* paddy and jute crops, floods occurring in late August or early September leave practically no time for replanting of rice seedlings. Appropriate planning that incorporates mid-flood season corrections in its mechanism can go a long way in remedy in this situation. Farmers usually face a shortage of seeds and seedlings to start fresh planting after the flood water recedes. The efforts could include a better mechanism to supply the appropriate seeds and seedlings immediately after the flood is over. This is over and above the fact that as extensive damages to the *Sali* paddy is by recurrent waves of floods, there is a immediate need to shift the emphasis from *kharif* to *rabi* crops and introduce multiple cropping in as many areas as possible. Restructuring of the cropping pattern is possible through the introduction of wheat, mustard, potato, lentil, summer mung. One commentator on the impact of floods in the state, arguing for the need for restructuring the cropping pattern in the state suggested following scheme.

Industrial Development

The availability of substantial deposits of natural resources like the alluvial plains of the Brahmaputra and Barak valleys, petroleum and natural gas, forests, coal, limestone etc., were adequate for providing a base for industrialisation, particularly for developing agro-based industries, petro-chemical complexes, gas-based units, etc., that could have at first served the requirements of the local-regional sections. Yet, the state reflects a scenario of economic backwardness-stagnation in agriculture and in industry today. This situation can be traced back the historical trends that in more than one way re-oriented the state's politico-economic perspective.

The pre-Colonial period was characterised by an agrarian economy, dominated by rice-culture. The state, as the core of the Ahom empire, was more or less self-sufficient and generated adequate surplus with which it was able to maintain its separate political status and trade. However, struggles for succession, regional power rivalry, the consequent expansion—devastation of the economy, and decimation of the population by the expanding Burmese power, completely transformed the regional scenario. The post-1826 period saw colonial consolidation of the area. It first restored the landscape and then introduced changes in the land use to meet the requirements of the colonial commercial and economic priorities. Two notable trends can be identified that influenced the transformation: These were: (i) the foundation of the economy, based on global economic process and trends, *i.e.*, introduction of plantation agriculture (Tea), economy and development of subsidiary ancillary industries to support the plantation. These were encouraged with a commercial and industrial bias, and, (ii) The initiation of processes that introduced the conversion of region to a primary product(s) producers/exporters, cultivating raw material requirements of the Colonial power.

The Colonial interest in the state was to ensure a sound raw material base on which the modern economy can function without any disruption of the source of supply. Typical to the exploitative character of the Metropolitan power, they were quick to seize the advantages of the ground conditions that afforded possibilities for tremendous commercial and economic gains. The outcome was the promotion of tea industry, jute cultivation on commercial basis, processing of crude oil and forest/wood products. The necessary prerequisite for such activities lay in the strengthening of the transport and communication linkages and network of economically viable regions of the state with the adjacent areas of the Ganga Delta. This introduced a trans-regional orientation and brought about a change. The latter were in terms of network of road and waterways, establishment of railways and introduction of postal and communication services on modern lines, all catering to the Colonial perspective of the economy.

Industrialisation in Assam is closely related with the development of tea plantation. Successful tea cultivation in Assam was realised in early 1830s. It began to flourish by 1859, when the Assam accompany with an area of 4,000 acres, produced about 0.17 million kg of tea annually. Area under tea expanded, so that by 1872,27,000 acres was brought under tea plantations in the state. These plantation produced 1.33 million kg annually. This industry was promoted by the State, which provided many incentives, such as, easy availability of waste land for tea cultivation, labour, enhancement of land revenue of other categories of land and grant of revenue free waste land for tea plantation, etc. These measures failed to elicit response from the local farmers. The problem of labour for plantation were overcome by import from other areas of the Sub-Continent. Petroleum is the single most important mineral resource. It has ample scope for encouraging industrialisation of the state. It was the Colonial power who initiated the processes of exploitation and processing and refining oil in Assam. Trial boring started in 1889. The Assam Oil Company was formed in 1899, and the Digboi Refinery was set up in 1901. The third major industry is the plywood industry. Like the Tea and the Petroleum, this was set up in 1918 with the setting up of the Assam Saw Mill and Timber Company and Assam Railway and Trading Company at Margherita in 1924.

It was during the early 1970s, that efforts were made to develop the down stream (Lower Brahmaputra overlay) industries with Bongaigaon as the focus. Assam has two well developed modern industries, viz. Tea and Oil. Besides, there are plywood units, Jute and sugar mills, the cement factory, the match factory etc. However, the number of medium and large-scale industries is not very large. As on 1990, there are only 88 large and medium scale industries in the State. Out of these 12 industries are in the central sector, 14 are in the estate sector and the rest are in the private sector. Since 1985–86 a number of new industrial units have come up. So that by 1993, there were 2402 registered factories. these can be grouped under following categories:

1. Agro-based industry: Tea industry, Food processing industry, Sugar industry and Textile.
2. Mineral-based industry: Metallic industry, Non-metallic industry, and Chemical industry.
3. Forest-based industry and
4. Miscellaneous

Regional Distribution

The industrial establishments in Assam are heavily concentrated in the district of Lakhimpur. Nearly 40 percent of the total industrial output of Assam comes from this district. More than 60 of every thousand of the population work in factories in this district compared to only seven out of every 1000 persons in the State as a whole. Dibrugarh, Tinsukia, Diboi, Makum, Marghariota, Namrup, Naharkatia,, are the important industrial towns located in a long belt by the side of the railway line. Doom Dooma and Moran are important centres of tea industry. With further development of oil and gas at Naharkatia, Duliajan and Moran, industrial activity in the region has the potential to grow further.

Sibsagar district has a rich tea industry. There were 253 gardens out of Assam's total of 746 gardens in 1962. Most of the gardens are located along the railway line from Barapathar to Namrup. The only sugar mill of Assam is located at Dergaon. Jorhat, Golaghat, Sibsagar, Mariani and Titabar are the important centres of industry. Mariani is developing a large plywood factory. Darrang district has no other industry except tea. It contains 97 gardens and these employ more than 95 percent of the factory labour in the district. A number of grain mills, mostly rice mills, have come up along the railway line from Khairabari to Rangapara. Tezpur with its relatively better facility of transport is the centre of agglomeration of industrial development in the district. Kamrup district is mainly an agricultural region. Tea industry is not very important in this district, only 15 tea gardens are located here.

Kamrup district is very well developed in agricultural processing and small-scale metal-based industries. Hajo and Sarthebari are the traditional centres of the bell-metal industry. Barpeta manufactures attractive ivory products. Nalbari is an important centre for the manufacture of Jhapi, a kind of hat made from bamboo and palm leaves. The district contains a large number of rice and oil mills, all located along the railway line. Other factories are largely concentrated in and around Guwahati, which has a unique location with regard to facilities by way of roads, railways, waterways and airways. With the establishment of the Industrial Estate, a large number of modern-sized industries have come up here. The location of the refinery at Noonmati has also generated a boom of industrial growth in the suburbs of the city, and as a result a large number of industrial units producing different types of utility goods have sprung up recently.

Nagaon district also contains a number of tea gardens and is rich in agriculture. So tea manufacturing and processing of agricultural products are two predominant industries absorbing four fifths of the industrial population. The Spun Silk Mill organised by the State Government is located at Jagiroad in this district. The proposed jute mill will also be located at Silghat on the bank of the river Brahmaputra. Hojai, Lanka and Jamunamukh are noted for their rice-mills. Cachar district in the Barak valley is another region of a big concentration of the tea industry contains 114 gardens.

According to the economic data available on the state for the period 1990–94, one can identify five districts in the category of the developed region; these comprise the districts of the Kamrup, Nagaon. Morigaon, Karimganj and Barpeta (4 in the Brahmaputra valley and one in the Barak valley). In the Brahmaputra valley, the developed districts form a compact area with more or less similar geomorphologically characteristics. Several factors are responsible for these districts to reach this position. In the region, modernisation of industries have played a key role for the area's development. Kamrup and Nagoan and Morigaon districts, in comparision to other districts in the state are industrially developed. The industrial activities are concentrated in major towns and cities. It has simultaneously led to high urbanisation, particularly after 1951.

Besides, city located in this area contributed a lion's share in the processes of development through industrialisation, accessibility, etc. This area has developed in agricultural sector. Barpeta and Nagapon have high cropping intensity and are dominant rice and jute producers in the state. They also have a high density of livestock and poultry population per km and high occupance in agriculture (persons per hectare of area sown). Besides, the area has comparatively better accessibility with other parts of the country. It has favourably developed infrastructural facilities, services, facilities and other socio-cultural amenities. Karimganj district in the Barak Valley has several factors that separate it from the rest in that part of the state. Being categorised as one of the developed areas of the state, it ranks second in the agricultural sector in the state. It has high cropping intensity (3rd in the state), high density of livestock and poultry population (2nd rank) and high percentage of utilisation of irrigation potential. In infrastructure, the district is well-developed (4th in the state). The areas with moderate level of development, is found in twelve districts that form four compact zones. These are found scattered in both the valleys: as in the southern upper Brahmaputra valley that includes the districts of Dibrugarh, Tinsukia, Sibsagar, Jorhat, Sonitpur and Darrang. The Nalbari district constututes another zone in the lower part of the Brahmaputra valley in the north Bank, while Goalpara, Bongaogaon and Dhubri districts in lower most part of the valley forms another micro-region of moderately developed region. Cachar and Hailakandi districts in the Barak valley also show such a level of development.

In Upper Assam, the moderately developed areas are characterised by oil-tea based industrial economy. This development has led to greater urbanisation; consequently have encouraged a comparatively more favourable infrastructural facilities. This zone has a high literacy rate than other districts in the valley (Jorhat, Sibsagar, Dibrugarh Districts rank first, third, fourth—in literacy rate in the state). However, it has been observed that this development in the middle and lower part of the Brahmaputra valley in the northern bank is attributed mainly to the dominant agricultural activity. These are obvious inferences one can draw from the fact that Darrang and Nalbari districts maintain their primacy (first and second position) in cropping intensity and (second and first) net area sown. Besides, Nalbari district tops in the density of livestock and poultry population per km in the state. These observations are also reinforced by the fact that this zone has a high road lengths per 100 km of area (Nalbari tops the rank in the state). The area is fairly well-developed in the basic infrastructural amenities. Goalpara, Bongaigaon and Dhubri Districts in the lower part of the Brahmaputra valley and the Cachar and Hailakandi districts in the Barak valley fall under this level of development and are characterised by dominant agricultural economy.

The districts of Lakhimpur, Dhemaji in the northern bank and Golaghat in the southern bank of the Brahmaputra valley come in the category of under-developed region. This zone is much behind other districts in agricultural, industrial activities and in infrastructural facilities. This can be partially explained by the fact that substantial area in these districts are more susceptible to incidence of floods and are also characterised by numerous turbulent tributaries like Subansiri in the right bank. Since the great earthquake of 1950, this region has been experiencing floods of varying intensities and of several waves. Such instances cause far-reaching consequences on the process of development in the state.

The two hill districts of Karbi Anglong and North Cachar Hills and Kokrajhar district in the lowermost part of the Brahmaputra valley form the backward area of the state. The hilly topography in addition to others of the region has altered the very process of desired level of development in agriculture, industry, infrastructure and others. On the other hand, the lack of industries, infrastructural and agriculture facilities have been the pivot factors for low development in the Kokrajhar district in the midst of substantially high density of population are indicators of factors that have entirely different implications. Suffice it to say here that this state of the zone's economy has enhanced the levels of alienation.

Assam is industrially backward in spite of its vast potential resource endowment. Even after about five decades of economic planning appreciable change in the industrial scenario have not occurred. Some positive signs have, however, been noticed in recent years. The industrial backwardness of Assam is due to a number of factors, which have been discussed in some details in appropriate places. Similar factors hampered many other states of the country at the time of Independence. But they have already overcome the difficulties and have progressed industrially. In Assam those factors still continue to play a dominant role in discouraging industrial development.

Problems of Further Administrative Re-orgaisation

The state reflected a complicated human landscape that had superimposition of traditions, backgrounds, priorities and interests. Because of its location and a long history of stability, the state of the Brahmaputra, Cachar Plains, Karbi Plateau complex, dominated the regional activities. It had the favourable geographical base to absorb many of the modernisation tendencies that emanated from its immediate boundaries. It enabled the territorially based traditional bureaucracy and elite pressure groups to continuously retain their hold on regional activity. Consolidation, change and commercialisation of activities influenced the power and position vis-à-vis other population groups and sub-groups. These were significantly transformed by moneterisation of the economy and spread of welfare measures including the development of language(s). This was followed by the emergence of distinct vocal sections among the native population, who through various organisation and cultural fora were able to restore the primacy of their culture (agitation to relocate the position of the Assamese in the 1860s and 1970s). This success increased their participation and representation; thereby, apart from the immigrant population, becoming the primary vehicle of socio-political transformation of the region.

On the other-hand, location of other population elements enforced isolation with activities of change dominated by the administrators and missionaries. These weak peripheries were characterised by general economic backwardness largely dominated by widespread shifting cultivation (along with its corresponding impact on structure and organisation), and poor communication facilities. As a result, their participation was confined to specific territories and subgroups with minimal interaction with others but more with the administrators. This enabled a separate perception to emerge among the different population groups and subgroups in the region—between the plains and the hill inhabitants, as also within the plains and hill inhabitants. Pre-1970, an agrarian economy was self-sustaining. These were developments indicating only the merger of interests but did not suggest the assimilation of identities. The latter surfaced with the widening of the cleavages and differences between the components of the population both in terms of participation and representation.

Disparities in resources were followed by inequalities in development of the state as a whole (within and outside). This coupled with the exposure to the process of change and impact of welfare measures activated the dormant divisive tendencies. The major population constituents like the Bodos, Karbis, etc., linked cultural identity with economic development and initiated socio-political movements towards attaining autonomy and control in the decision-making processes. So that, in the state, the competition and confrontation of divergent interests were focussed around the majority group, the immigrant group and the minority groups, spread over across the east-west direction in the state. Interestingly, movements were largely represented by the student elements. This phenomena became prominent only in the late 1950s and early 1960s. This closely followed the diverse groups and sub-groups efforts towards individual cultural identification and their respective notions of nationality. It was frequently assumed that the dominant language grew at the cost of the other language dialects.

REFERENCES

1. H.P. Das (1970), *Geography of Assam*, NBT, New Delhi.
2. R. Gopalakrishnan (1991), *North-East: Land, Economy and* People, Har Anand-Vikas, New Delhi.
3. R. Gopalakrishnan (2000), *Assam: Land and People*, Omsons, New Delhi.
4. *North-East Geographer*, North-Eastern India Geographical Society, Department of Geography, Guahati University, Guwahati, articles on Assam in the Journal volumes from 1986 onwards.

CHAPTER 1

Assam—Brahmaputra Valley and the Hill Districts

This chapter deals issues that have been identified as areas that require a detailed research, and have been presented the way the various discussants wanted it to be. These are divided in the following sections:

1. RESEARCH PRIORITIES IN SOCIAL SCIENCES FOR THE 90S FOR ASSAM

—*Farida Ahmed Das*

One of the main aims of any science is its usefulness in the service of mankind. As such its applied or 'practical' aspect should be emphasised than the needs of mankind. The first criterion for the selection of new research projects should be to serve the interest of the people. In the light of the present day context some problem-oriented research works of value to the people are necessary for effective formulation and implementation of development programmes. The findings of such research works should be popularised.

I would like to draw attention to few areas of research that may be taken up on a priority basis for the 90s.

North eastern region of India is famous for its diverse ethnic groups. People belonging to different socio-economic classes and for different linguistic groups were living together. But in recent times in a changed political and economic condition a great deal of conflict and tension among the different ethnic groups is quite apparent. To understand this problem and to find out the various factors and forces that may be responsible for such development, detailed micro level studies are not only necessary but I feel should get priority. In this context basic informations on historical, cultural and linguistic affinities, social structure, socio-cultural belief will be of great importance. There are instances of migration and of intercultural exchange. Ethno-historic study of biological nature may help in understanding the relationship of the different ethnic groups and building up of national harmony.

As students of social biology, we feel it necessary in carrying out researches aimed at improvement of health and nutrition, prevention of diseases, maintenance of normal growth and also to deal with the population problem in India.

Some research projects may be planned to investigate the impact of different socio-cultural and economic factors on health and nutritional status of different populations in the north east. Child care practices and infant and child mortality rate in different populations may be studied. Frequency of different diseases and also of deficiency condition in the different groups should be worked out. Problem and possible menace of AIDS should also be considered.

Population problem, which is a major concern of the population experts, is another field that draws attention. A biologist role in the study of population problem is to measure the differential fertility of the different groups of people. Demography offers immense scope for research in the aspect of population growth. Demographic structure of a population can be useful not only for understanding socio-cultural aspect but also useful for interrupting important features like fertility, infant and child mortality, population composition, sex ratio etc.

There have been very few studies on demography and fertility in the region.

Study on age at menarche can also be of great importance. This biological phenomenon has got relevances in the study of fertility performances and physical growth. Some social law mainly those relating to marriage can be and should be made on the menarcheal age. It has been found by many investigations that the average menarcheal age of the girls are gradually going down. It may ultimately have an effect on fertility.

The different socio-economic and cultural factors that may influence on this biological phenomenon may be looked into.

Another field of study that may concern the social scientist is the impact of family planning programmes in the population, which has got relevance to fertility.

The national family planning programme started in 1951, which mainly aimed at reducing birth rate to plan family. The family planning programme has made a significant impact on fertility. Various studies show that fertility of city women are mainly affected by the birth control practices. Thus a secular trend in the fertility performance is evident. It is high time to investigate the sociological as well as biological consequences of family planning methods. Whatever efforts the policy maker has made to popularise the programme it has yet to reach the less educated and economically backward classes. Therefore if population is decreasing due to adoption of family planning methods it is time to see what type of people are decreasing. It may have ill effect on the social health in the long run.

One important point where I want to emphasise is duration for the mass people. Education has become a matter of great importance and Government and other organisation have made tremendous effort to make the people educated. As socio-economic factors play important roles in successful implementation of educational programmes for a society, social scientists automatically come into picture. I feel there is a need for greater and better integration of educational programme within the socio-cultural and economic condition of the people at the policy making level as well as implementation level. Some studies may be planned to look into the type and methods of education, minimum age for admission, contents and medium of instruction and their relevance to different socio-economic condition.

Finally I feel an integrated and inter disciplinary approach is necessary to understand the different social, cultural, economic, psychological, sociological and political problems of the people of north eastern India. Attempt should be made to systematise the techniques and to establish the kinds of study needed for north east India on priority basis.

2. AREAS OF ANTHROPOLOGICAL RESEARCH

—*R.K. Kar*

According to 1991 Census, the total population of North-East India is about 31 million who are distributed over an area of about 2,55,000 sq. km. The region is a cultural corridor between India and South East Asia. It is of strategic importance (in terms of geography, history, demography and culture).

A. Because of its unique location, population composition and terrain, this region may be regarded as a laboratory for researches in various social sciences, where different theories, could be tested and new ideas given graphic accounts.

B. Traditional arts and crafts of various tribes be properly documented.

C. Tribal studies can be planned to incorporate the process of change.

D. Various tribal groups have been seen trying to come to grips with the problems of defining and externalising new linkages with other neighbouring groups, the regional society, the nation-state and ultimately the outside world as a whole. Ethnic-cultural identity has also been found to be increasingly used as a resource for mobilising the people in socio-political spheres. Some studies may be planned in this direction to understand the on-going tribal unrest in this region.

The People and the Ecosystem

Investigations be planned on cultural, social and economic fronts of particular communities forming a part of the total ecosystem. Thus, for example, there are some areas like.

A. Man and River

What happens to the riverine villages when the equilibrium is lost due to flood, erosion, shifting course, shifting or due to human intervention such as construction of dams for generating hydel power and irrigation projects, discharge of effluents into the river etc.

The character and tenor of adaptation of man to these riverine calamities and also to modern water-shed management programmes may be investigated.

B. Man and Forest

(i) Interaction between man (as a dependent agent) and forest (as a supplier of resources) is well known. The serious consequences of deforestation are also well known. Some studies may be planned in this problem area. This is a unique kind of man-nature interaction. The patterns of land and habitat resource management and their consequences on the eco-system may be investigated.

(ii) There are thousands of Tibetan refugees in Miao and Bordumsa areas of Tirap district, Arunachal Pradesh. Possibilities of social tension between settlers and indigenous tribals apart, the fairly sudden settlement of immigrants, even if in a planned and government-aided programme, to a new and hitherto pristine ecological setting is likely to generate a series of changes, both on the human and the physical environmental fronts. A study of adaptation of the Tibetans to the new setting as well as ecological implications of the settlements may be made.

C. Endemic Diseases and the Eco-system, as well as the Social Security Services Available in the Backward Areas

D. Shifting Cultivation and the Eco-system

3. AREAS OF ANTHROPOLOGICAL RESEARCH

—*Bapukan Choudhury*

Men's relationship with nature is a complicated and many-sided problem. The association of human society with the nature, whose practices tend to change over time and space, exposes man to varied environmental condition. Today we, in North-East India, are at a stage of vast changes. These changes are affecting the distribution, population density and way of life of the communities of this region. It is certain that many relatively soon be totally transformed, we are, therefore, in a period when the biology and culture of the people of this region are undergoing continuous change. In view of this, the following research areas may be recommended for urgent attention.

Health and Nutrition

Health is considered as the wealth of a nation. The urgent need for the improvement of the health status especially for women, children and underprivileged groups is felt at present by all nations of the world. In the absence of a planned physical growth surveys, it is difficult to understand the progress in health and nutritional status of an area. If we are to provide health for all by 2000 A.D., we must have to know the level of malnutrition among different communities of the region. Malnutrition is the biggest public health problem in our country today. Nutritional deficiency diseases account for considerable proportion of hospital admissions. But considering the wide range of regional, ecological, ethnic, socio-economic and cultural variations, we know very little about the physical growth and then the nutritional status of the people of this region.

An intensive and extensive survey of the physical growth and the level of malnutrition among the different population groups demands immediate attention of the Social Scientists of this region. This is one of the areas where both physical and cultural anthropologists can work together. Because growth and nutritional status is very much dependent on the overall integrated development of a society measured in terms of cultural, technological, economic, educational, social and political situation.

Demographic Studies

Demographic study is another area that needs immediate attention of the social scientists of this region. The success of a particular group of individual in a particular set of environmental condition is observable in terms of the group's age and sex structure, distribution, change in size etc. One method of examining a group's ecological success is to determine its demographic response to change in physical/biotic/social environment. The absolutely necessary condition for ecological success is survival of a group over time.

In man, culture conditions the interaction with the environment. In recent times penetration of market economy into the traditional economic system has caused radical social changes. There is change in activity, food type, disease sectors etc. as the penetrating market economy changes the labour patterns, reliance upon local versus long distance resources, medical technology etc. In order to maintain the ecological perspective, cultural factors must be rephrased in ecological terms. With the encounter of traditional populations by the expanding social systems, new social and economic patterns emerge by which previously isolated groups are incorporated into more complex social entities. Under this situation fertility may or may not change for some time. However, fertility is likely to decline to the level of mortality as new niches become filled. At the same time, the new social and economic patterns may disrupt the traditional aspirations, values and world view and change the perception of the state of being or quality of life.

The maternal age, parity and birth interval are important intermediate variable through which social and economic determinate operate to influence the fertility and the risk of infant and child mortality and morbidity. There are lot of other factors like birth spacing, marriage patterns, beliefs and practices which can influence fertility and mortality rates. These variables differ from culture to culture. Assam as well as the rest of the states in the region provide adequate scope to examine the effect of different cultural factors on the fertility, mortality and morbidity. The findings of the studies in this time will help not only in providing the guidelines for solving the burning population problem of the nation but also in formulating welfare measures for the different societies.

Migration Studies

In recent years there is large scale immigration and immigration to different North-East Indian states. This has resulted the change in biology and culture of the people of this region. The nature and direction of change is, however, yet to be explored. This particular aspect needs to be studied very urgently.

4. PRIORITY AREAS IN ANTHROPOLOGY

—A.N.M. Irshad Ali

Culture and Ecology: The Indigenous Vision

Terms like ecological development, ecological system, ecological balance, etc., are practically in every bodies lips these days both at regional and global level. There have been discipline specified approaches to these problems and at times even multidisciplinary approaches are also evident. But in these approaches mostly 'outside' experts are involved to tackle issues and settle problems of 'inside' natives.

It is a known fact that ecology plays a vital role in conditioning and culture of a given area and that geographical situation of a locale goes a long way in shaping the needs, custom, behaviour and thought of the people. Anthropologists put great emphasis in taking into consideration every factor that affects man's life and culture. Hence, it is but natural that anthropologists are also interested in the study of ecology in general and the intimate relationship between culture and its surrounding environment in particular.

Any general attempt to understand the ecological relationships and its problems tends to remain partial if the native or participants point of view on these issues are not taken into consideration. Because the participants of each culture have their distinctive ways of perceiving the environment. Every human group has their own explanations of the environment which are reflected in their tales, proverbs, beliefs and customs and in the language of the people.

An understanding of the 'indigenous vision' of environment is of great importance in that it gives clues to comprehend how people have worked out the ways to cope with environmental problems and also the kind of balance brought to the environment through various indigenous culture mechanisms. In view of this, the need for understanding the 'indigenous vision' cannot be overemphasised. It may perhaps be stated that such an effort helps in perceiving issues at the grass root level. This in turn will help in assessing the needs and aspirations of the local people.

It appears that in the context of development, anthropologists can provide immense help to various development agencies and organisations whose primary concern are the issues relating to ecological development. In this context anthropologists can provide with an in-depth view of environment of the level of actual empirical reality. This will require the involvement the anthropologists in the research of this sort. Their view points will also have to be adequately given weightage by development agencies and organisations. It is felt that the expectations behind development could be better fulfilled provided the general approaches to ecological development join hand with the anthropological approach to understand the relationship between the culture and ecology.

Urban Research in Assam: Anthropological Approach

From Anthropological point of view there is need to undertake empirical research in the Assam region with a view to understand some of the basic issues centring urbanisation and urban life in Assam region. Anthropological research in Assam region pertaining to urban situations needs to focus on some of the areas outlined below :

The network of relations between rural and urban inhabitants and the on going rural urban link, pull and push factors involved in migration. The quality and content of socio-cultural life of recently migrated rural people to the towns and city. Transportation of tradition from village to towns, and nature of adjustment of rural migrants to town and city life, also the settlement pattern of the migrants in the towns and city and the nature and function of kinship and family in urban situations. It also includes inter-ethnic relations, problems of health, education and poverty in urban situations as well as the role of history in designing the characters of towns and city in Assam region.

Anthropological research in the above areas promises to help in understanding the phenomena of urbanisation and urban life in Assam region. Such research, which obviously would be holistic in nature (that is to say the perception of an aspect in its setting) also promises the understanding of the part and whole relationship. The complexity and the quality and content of life of the urban communities generally constitute some amount of difficulty in applying the methods and techniques of anthropology to the study of urban communities. At the same time, many anthropologists have also demonstrated that they can approach the urban communities with the basic methodology of classical anthropology.

Understanding Inter-ethnic Relations in Assam

North-East India including Assam is a region of wide ethnic diversity. The population of Assam is distributed through a large number of tribal and non-tribal ethnic groups. The nature of ethnic diversity of Assam has also been augmented by the migration of peoples to this region from the ancient to the present time. Migrations to this region have also resulted spectacular social transformations. Furthermore, the process of interaction between the cultures of the migrants and those of the autochthonous have resulted in the growth of a few ethnic groups like the Assamese Muslims, Assamese Sikhs etc. Many such ethnic groups exist in the wider Assamese Society as inseparable and non-isolated entities. Their cultures operate within the social structure as segments of a common social system.

In a situation as outlined above, there is obvious need for scientific exploration of the nature of various ethnic groups and their inter-relationships in order to understand the cooperation, completion and conflict among different ethnic groups. Inter-ethnic tensions and conflicts often erupt in pasts of the country involving various groups. It is reasonable to expect that empirical studies delineating the nature of intra inter-group relations and linkages can provide us with facts for a better understanding of the situation rather what would be obtained through generalised observations.

5. COMMERCE WITH SPECIAL REFERENCE TO ASSAM

—A.R.M. Rehman

According to Francis Rummel, "Research is careful inquiry or examination to discover new information or relationships and to expand and to verify existing knowledge." Social research studies man and his institutions. It is largely empirical. Social research is bound to be inter-disciplinary as the social phenomena are not isolated.

Business research is essentially an investigation and an analysis of business situations in the changing environment for the purpose of providing information for the growth and expansion of the business. The relevance of business research is far greater in developing countries like India which are confronted with complex socio-economic problems like poverty, unemployment, underemployment, illiteracy and the like.

Research Programme already Completed

Doctoral research themes that were carried out in Commerce in Assam are Economic Development of Assam are, Industrial Development of Assam, Agricultural Marketing in Assam, Tea Marketing in Assam, Problems and Prospects of Small-scale Industries, Handloom Industries of Assam, on the role of Central Finance in the Economic Development of Arunachal Pradesh, the Marketing of Assam Tea with special reference to the Dibrugarh District, Capital Taxation in India, Income, Savings and Investment of the Mishing Tribal Community of Upper Assam.

6. RESEARCH PRIORITIES IN COMMERCE IN ASSAM

—A.R.M. Rehman

In Commerce, research may be undertaken in different areas like Accounting Financial Management, Marketing, Human Resource Management, Taxation, Banking, Trade and Transport.

The following are some of the issues, which should be accorded due priorities for research in Assam.

Public Enterprises in Assam

There are 44 public enterprises in Assam. The total capital invested in public enterprises which includes share capital, long term borrowings, Capital subsidy and grants and subsidies which was Rs. 483.20 crores in 1980–81 rose to Rs. 1,124.61 crores in 1986–87.

The total Govt. investment (as share capital, grants, loans and subsidies) in public enterprises was Rs. 712.63 crores in 1986–87. Of the total investment made by the Govt. investment in the ASEB, ASTC and the Assam Tea Corporation Ltd. alone accounted for 70.66 percent of the total investment in 1986–87. The turnover in all the public enterprises in the state, which was Rs. 101.66 crores in 1980–81 increased to Rs. 282.18 crores in 1986–87. The total employment in public enterprises in the state increased from 48,168 in 1980–81 to 53,360 in 1986–87.

The ratio of turnover to employment, which is an index of labour productivity, shows that the overall average figure for all the public enterprises in the state which was Rs. 021 lakh/employees in 1980–81 rose to Rs. 0.53. lakh/employees in 1986-87. The financial performance of the public enterprises in Assam has been very dismal. 24 out of 44 public enterprises incurred losses amounting to Rs. 9.231.33 lakhs in 1986–87. Only 11 enterprises earned profit.

Public enterprises in the state are running at losses. Consequently, there is a need of the hour to undertake research on the various aspects of the working of these organisations so as to diagnose the weaknesses and shortcomings and to suggest remedial measures for revitalising these public enterprises in the greater interest of the people of Assam. Considering the losses incurred by the ASEB, ASTC, the Assam Tea Corporation Ltd. And the STATFED it has become necessary to undertake research on these organisations before it becomes too late to bring them back to the rail.

Industrial Productivity and Profitability

Researchers be encouraged to undertake to study on the productivity and profitability of major industries of Assam and to suggest measures for the improvement of the same.

Entrepreneurship Development

This is another area in which research studies may lead to uncover many phenomena concerning Entrepreneurship Development.

7. RESEARCH NEEDS OF VILLAGE & SMALL INDUSTRY SECTOR

—D.D. Mali

This note is prepared to discuss about the research needs for the development of Village and Small Industry (VSI) Sector with particular reference to North-Eastern Region. The discussion is confined to identification of potential areas for research in the VSI sector. The purpose of this note is, therefore, specific and limited to one area of concern. The VSI Sector has been assigned an important role in the national economy. In order to develop this sector various policy measures have been adopted and support provided. Institutional infrastructure have been created and development programmes adopted. As a result the VSI sector has grown over the years. Particular mention may be made of the SSI sector, which has made tremendous progress during the last two decades or so. But the development of SSI Sector in N-E Region is slow. As on December 1990 the region had 25,525 registered SSI units, according to 1.9 percent of the total SSI units in the country. As per the second All India Census of SSI units, out of 12395 units (as on March 1988 in N-E Region from where data could be collected) 9330 units were working and 3065 units were closed units. The percentage of closed units is 24.7. Out of 9330 units, Assam had 4430 units.

The slow growth of VSI Sector in the region was due to a number of inhibiting factors—infra-structural, finance, raw material, marketing, taxation, organisational, entrepreneurial etc. These problems have been identified and remedial measures suggested by various committees, working groups, conferences. The Sivaraman Committee (1988) the conference of Industry Ministers of the States and Union Territories of NER (July, 1981), standing committee of the All-India SSI Board or the development of small industries in NLR, NISIET study (1978) discussed the constraints and prospects of Industrial Development, and recommended the strategies for the development of industries, particularly village and small scale industries in the region.

Though various committees, working groups and conferences had suggested various measures for the development of VSI Sector yet the region continue to be industrially backward. In the context of the development—one is training and another is research. In order to identify the training needs specific studies are required so that tailor-made training programme can be taken up either for upgradation of specific skill or for development of motivation among the prospective entrepreneurs. The concern of this note is not identification of training needs. The concern is on identification of research needs.

The broad areas of research for village and small industries may be grouped under infrastructure, ancillary development, various aspects of management, promotional organisations and their role, programmes for development of village and Small Industry Sector, and their impact, sickness in small industry sector, development of entrepreneurship including developing entrepreneurship among women. There are several of these areas where research has not been done or if some research has been done more needs to be done. Infrastructural facilities are pre-requisite for industrial development. In order to plan the type of industries for development in a particular place/district it is necessary to have adequate information regarding infrastructural facilities actually available in that particular area. It is sometime misleading to go by the statistic regarding the availability of infrastructural facilities, particularly power, transport and communication facilities. It is better to have amenities survey to ascertain the availability of the required amenities and facilities in the district or a sub-division to plan for the development of village and small industries.

There are a number of programmes launched by the Government for providing infrastructural facilities. Among these programmes Industrial Estate Programme is an important one. This programme was launched during the later part of the First Five Year Plan with a view to provide all types of facilities required by the small scale unit in an Industrial Estate. It is necessary to make a study regarding the impact of Industrial Estate Programme on the development of small scale industry with particular reference to any of the State or of the region as whole. Some study on the programme of Industrial Estate Programme was made by the Evaluation and Monitoring

Division of the Planning and Development Department of the Government of Assam. This was in the nature of looking into the existing status of the Industrial Estate Programme. Another study was made by the Vejpa Committee on the Industrial Estate of the North-Eastern Region. But none of these studies aimed at assessing the impact of Industrial Estate Programme on the development of small scale industries and entrepreneurship.

In the region there are 155 large and medium scale industries. Assam has 116 large and medium scale industries. But the number of ancillary industries are hardly thirty. There are prospects for development of ancillary industries based on the requirements of large and medium scale industries. The industries which offer scope for maximum ancilliarisation needs to be studies and strategies for ancillary development, for promoting first generation entrepreneurs is to be adopted.

The District Industries Centres have been operating in the respective States of the region for the last more than a decade. The District Industries Centres are primarily responsible for the development of VSI Sector. It is necessary to closely examine the role of the District Industries Centres in promoting entrepreneurship in the VSI Sector. In addition to the District Industries Centres there are Small Industry Development Corporations or Industrial Development Corporations, set up to act as catalyst for the development of small industry sector. It is necessary to study the roles of these corporations in promoting small sector industries. For the development of village industries there are Handloom and handicrafts Development Corporations, for Khadi and Village Industries Board, for Electronic Industries, Electronic Development Corporations for Textile Industries, Textile Corporation etc. Case studies of a few of these corporations will be helpful in formulating policies for development of specific type of industries in the region.

The banks and financial institutions are to play the role of friends, philosophers and guide. It has however, been observed that they have largely failed in this respect. A general complaint of the VSI entrepreneurs is that banks are more security minded and not development oriented. Research studies conducted in this respect has also revealed that banks are more security minded. Banks, on the other hand state that they are willing to lend to the SSI Sector but there are no worthwhile proposal. Some studies have been done by research scholars on the role of banks in providing finance to the SSI Sector. But such studies have obvious limitations due to time and resource constraint of individual researchers. In order to have a proper understanding of the role of banks in providing finance to the SSI Sectors, a comprehensive study is required.

The N-E Region accounts for less than 2 percent of the total small scale industries in the country. But it accounts for around 7 percent of the total sick SSL Units in the country. The causes of industrial sickness as per a 'Note' circulated by the Reserve Bank in a SLIIC Meeting for units enjoying credit limit of Rs. 1 lakh and above at the end of December, 1987 pointed out that 89 percent of industrial sickness in N-E Region was due to management deficiency. The second All-India Census of SSI Units, however, reveal that 40 percent of the units in N-E Region were closed due to problem of finance and not due to management deficiency. In view of this it is necessary to make a study of the problems of industrial sickness in N-E Region.

Related to industrial sickness there are researchable areas relating to rehabilitation scheme and turned around strategies. This will be only case studies. There are other areas needing research which may be in the nature of evaluation study for programmes of self-employment, TRYSEM and similar other programme launched by the Government for the promotion of village and small industry in the country in general and in N-E Region in particular.

The areas suggested in this note is only illustrative in nature and not exhaustive. In fact, no note can be made fully exhaustive on the needs of research for village and small industry sector. This note however, shows a number of areas where research can be undertaken for the benefit of the region.

8. THE INFORMAL SECTOR

—Mini Bhattacharyya Thakur

In our present day world there is the need to concentrate on a few questions at a time and there is the temptation to delve deeper into some limited issues and forget the broader ones. In this paper, I have dealt with the Informal Sector (IFS) at large and some important issues of research in this sector relevant to the North-East India. The economy of the developing countries can be characterised by the distinction between the modern and the traditional sectors which John Keith Hart calls the Formal and Informal sector. These terms are also interchangeably called as organised and unorganised. The Formal sector is after the consequence of foreign investment and western technology and the Informal sector is the large volume of self employed in a developing country who are engaged in small scale labour intensive work such as tailoring, food preparation trading, shoe repairing, etc. These people are often regarded as unemployed or under-employed as they cannot be included in national employment statistics but they are often highly productive and make significant contribution to national income. Some of the important features of this sector are:

Easy of Entry

The industries are family or cottage industries using resources locally, size of operation is small, labour intensive, workers are unskilled and acquire skills through an on the job training, IFS activities develop without government support, working conditions are deplorable and low wages. The reverse is the case of the Formal sector. They are characterised by: difficulty of entry, legal form of industries depending on imported raw material or machinery, large-scale and having regulated markets, capital intensive techniques, skilled and professional trained workers.

The Case for the IFS

The case for the IFS become stronger as the debate concerning the characteristics and significance of small scale employment outside the modern organised sector began to produce implications. Cases of how working poor survive has opened a new chapter of development planning. The viability and expansion of this sector with easy entry, failure of the organised/formal sector to provide adequate employment, factors like land over population; low agricultural productivity and rural-urban migrations play an important part in the expansion of this sector.

In some of the more developed countries particularly in the Socialist East Europe where practically everybody is fully employed and within the formal sector, there is at present a growing demand for small services like washing of clothes, shoe repairing and shining, hawking and vending of petty things etc. In the present situation because of rising unemployment and growing inflation, the people with fixed income are the most affected and would prefer to supplement their income through these small activities. But, the socialist ideology against exploitation of labour (that of exploitative linkage between FS and IFS, low wages and low selling prices of goods) did not favour the growth of this IFS. However, changes in the attitude of the people and development of market ethos are the welcome factors for the growth of the IFS (personal communication, Dr. Gautam Mazumdar, January, 1993). Whatever the outcome of the debate might be, one thing is clear that the IFS is here to stay and it not only provides employment but also essential commodities and services for rich and poor alike in cities everywhere, in developed, developing and centrally planned economics (Mathur and Moser, 1984). Particularly depend on these services and goods provided by the IFS are the urban poor who could not afford them otherwise (Schmink, 1986).

Issues

The earlier writings on formal/informal dualism tended to create a division between these two sectors which obscure their interconnections and interdependencies. It is therefore pertinent to identify some of the current issues of research in this important field of IFS to lend clarity and definition. Some of the important issues are: To identify the linkages between FS and IFS—The critical issues here would be to identify the activities undertaken by individuals, households and work communities. Secondly, the urban IFS's linkages with the rural IFS. Primarily through seasonal, permanent and temporary migration. Thirdly the interdependence of both the sectors in the use of raw materials, recycling, use of bye-products and small manufacturing by the home-based units in the IFS. Investigate unrecorded urban economic activity to find out the type of employment, activities—temporary or permanent, benign or exploitative, transitory or permanent, etc., women and IFS. In developing countries where the line between home craft and home-based work is blurred, home based work has continued to be a major economic activity. In these activities women are actively involved but the work done by women in their home by and large remains invisible. These should be enumerated and analysed.

The Relationship between City Size and the IFS

Detailed study on the concentration of IFS activities, urban city based, rural or small towns. Their distinctive activities, type of employment, people and culture and the type of rural micro-enterprises.

Anthropology and Informal Sector Research

Anthropology as the scientific study of man has spread its tentacles to the study of almost all the aspects of the life of man. Its confines are not only limits to simple non-western scientists, culture and economy but have also developed methodological principles in the study of urban life. By the end of the 1990s, more than half the world's six billion people will live in cities and twenty of those cities will house more than eleven million each. The proportion of city dwellers will slope upwards even further in the next century. In view of the increasing importance of the city as on nerve centre of activity, it would be interesting to study urban life and culture, work pattern, dualism of economy, economic activities, survival and social existence.

Anthropology, with its methodology of primary fieldwork, coupled with qualitative enquiry and quantitative surveys will be in a better position to analyse the IFS and the people. However as interdisciplinary approach combing economists, human geographers, psychologists and anthropologists would be a better prospect.

IFS Research in North-East India

Research in the IFS in the N-E India is very limited. One important study sponsored by the SBI was conducted by Dr. Phani Deka which is worth-mentioning. This study looked into the financial and credit needs of the small entrepreneurs in the IFS in the city of Guwahati. However, new research studies are being conducted in this field. But there is still a big lacuna in IFS studies which must be filled to get a comprehensive picture of the IFS scenario in the North-Eastern India.

9. THE SOCIO-ECONOMIC STATUS, PROBLEMS AND PROSPECTS OF THE AREA UNDER BODOLAND AUTONOMOUS COUNCIL: Geo-Economic Study

—M. Taher

The area proposed to be transferred to the BAC lies among the Himalayan foothills in the north Brahmaputra plain. Physiographically, the area includes, by and large, bhabar and tarai belts supporting in semi-evergreen forests and tall grassland. Agriculture and lumbering are the two main primary occupations of the inhabitants, other economic activities being singularly absent so far, except a score of large and small tea plantations owned by people from outside the area. The infrastructure for economic development is absent. The total population of the area is estimated at about 14 lakhs distributed over slightly more than 2000 villages and a mere 4 or 5 towns. If the area is to come up as a viable politico-economic unit of the people for whom it has been created, it would be necessary to undertake measures for its development right earnest. And, for this purpose, a through demographic and socio-economic study is of utmost necessity. An outline of the study may be visualised as follows:

Geographical Basis:	Identification of the area and boundary. Physiography, behaviour of the rivers, soil types and natural vegetation.
Population:	Study of total number, Growth, Distribution and Density, Settlement Pattern, Social Groups, Age-Sex Structure, Literacy, Occupational Pattern, Rural-Urban Composition, etc.

Resources:	Study of land resources and limitations, Forest resource, Any other resource.
Resource Utilisation:	Study of Agriculture, Lumbering, Cottage Industry, Trade and Commerce, Transport and Communication, Other Services, etc.
Perception and Welfare:	Study of the aspirations of the people which led them to launch the agitation, and suggesting the basis of the findings above (considering the problems and prospects) how best these can be met and a continuous process of development initiated.

10. INDUSTRY AND COMMERCE

—D. Bhorali and K. Baura

Evaluation of Public Expenditure and its Impact on Economic Development of Assam

In this topic an examination on the pattern of Government expenditure under different heads during the last decade may be carried out. Social and economic overheads are the most important ingredients for the economic development in a socialistic economy. An econometric analysis through statistical technique would help to achieve the object of this study.

A Study on the Measurement of Government Revenue and its Administration in Assam

An analytical survey may be carried on the different sources of Government revenue in Assam. Scope of increasing both tax and non revenue in the State be examined. The problem of collection of revenue and its administration will be covered for the measurement of revenue in the state of Assam.

Performance of Public Sector Undertakings in Assam

Performance of Public Sector undertaking in the State is quite unsatisfactory. An attempt may be made to ascertain the causes of dismal performance of the P.S. units. Emphasis may be given on the aspects as to how these units may be made viable and thus contribute to the overall economic Development of the State.

An Economic Analysis of Public Enterprises—A Break Even Analysis

Public enterprises are the main economic units of the Government along with its services motive. An economic analysis will be made on its performance through break even analysis. The variable and fixed components of cost are the main variable for break even analysis. This analysis would show the real practice through which it could be survived. In this study the main emphasis will be on the cost structure of the public enterprises.

Performance Appraisal of Public Transport System in Assam. The Study may be Confined to the Performance of the State Transport Corporation

The basis of decision making and accounting information relating to its activities would be covered to find out its present deficiencies.

Road Transport System (Other than ASTC) of the State

A study on the various Road Transport System (both passenger and goods) operating in the State may be undertaken. Rural and Urban Road transport system may be taken up in a phased manner.

Cost Benefit Analysis of Poverty Alleviation Programmes in Assam

As huge amount of money has been spent by the Government for rural development and alleviation of rural poverty, now it is a time to see whether this spending could create any asset for the rural poor. It is therefore necessary to have a survey on the money spent for rural poverty alleviation programmes in our country.

Status of Home-Workers

Study on the working condition, wage pattern and status of the house-maids and boy's working urban households.

Working Condition of Child Labourer

Child workers engaged in construction work, factory and workshops may form subject-matter of such study. Mode of appointment, working condition, monthly salary or daily wage paid to these workers, hours of work, etc. will throw light on the neglected section.

A Study of Regional Rural Bank—Their Role in Rural Development in Assam

Regional Rural banks are created as the primary financing institutions to operate in the rural areas. After a decade of their functioning in the rural areas, it is now essential to evaluate their role in rural development and to examine their problems in financing rural development. A field study in the operating areas and credit deposit ratio of the bank will help to evaluate their functioning.

Role of Informal Sector in Urban Economy

In this study an overall economic structure of the urban area is to be analysed. Unorganised or Informal sector is one of the growing areas to contribute sufficient amount to the Gross National Product of the State. It would be the endeavours to examine their role as an economic unit in the urban economy. A socio-economic survey in the urban areas help much to understand the working of this sector.

Analysis of Capital Investment in Registered Small Scale Sector

The growth and development of small scale industry is considered as an element for generation of employment and it helps in the process of industrialisation in the country. A survey would speak its activity and capital investment in this sector for future decision making by the concerned authorities. Besides these, emerging horizon of the Secondary Sector in Developing Social Responsibility, Urban Resource Development Expectation and Possibilities, Industrial Policies Since Independence, Accounting As A Tool of Resource Mobilisation and Allocation Envioeloping Economic, are also important.

Status of Working Women

Women engaged in different establishments, and organisations, their status vis-a-vis male counterpart—mode of conveyance to their place of work—problem of accommodating for single working women etc. will reveal interesting reading.

Unorganised Rural Markets. Weekly or fortnightly 'Bazars' or 'hats' will be an interesting subject matter or study rural markets are a feature of our rural economy. The heterogeneous products ranging from textiles, to food products, are being traded in this markets.

Performance Evaluation and Practices in a Professionally Managed Enterprise and a Family Run Enterprise—A Comparative Study, A Study of Training Effectiveness of State Bank of India—Assam Region, Voluntary Disclosure Process in India with Special Reference to Industry. Organisational Climate and Leadership, Effectiveness of Financial and Non Financial Incentives as Motivators for Sales Personnel, Financing through IFCI and ICICI: A Comparative Study, Entrepreneurial Competence as Determinant of Entrepreneurial Success—North-East India Content, Liquidity Analysis through Ratio and Cash Flow in some Industries.

11. THE STUDY OF PUBLIC ENTERPRISES

—S.B. Baruah and N.N. Sarma

The policy framework for the growth of the public sector was specially declared by the Govt. of India in the shape of two Industrial Policy Resolutions, the first one in 1948 and the second in 1956. In subsequent policy recommendations the expansion of Public Sector was advanced for three reasons—to gain control of the commanding heights of the economy; to promote critical development strategic value rather than priority on considerations of project; to provide commercial surpluses to finance further economic development.

In conformity with the National Policy the States of North-East have promoted a large number of Public Sector Enterprises during the past three decades. Today, these state level public enterprises cover a wide variety of organisations and institutions ranging from those which are commercially oriented to those directed towards providing social benefits and with others falling between the two extremes. Today, these enterprises assume a major role in the economic and social development of the region.

Performance of PSE's has been a subject matter of discussion at all levels. The North-Eastern Enterprises are also no exception to this. Despite assigning a very important role to the PE's and providing all co-operation and support for the development of the PE's the performance of the SLPE's in North-East is very discouraging. The size of the public sector as well as the complexity of the overall management and monitoring system varies from state to state in accordance with their socio political system. Since the motives for the establishment an existence of PE's are socio-economically conditioned, their performance cannot be measured with the same criterion as private enterprises. It must be measured not only by financial profitably but also on the basis of their contribution to the general well being of society as a whole and other aspects of performance. A pertinent issue, therefore arises in the context of the wider interest of the economy whether Public Enterprises should be allowed to be managed by private sector talent. The concept of inviting private sector talent to manage public enterprise when these enterprises are not efficient in their performance is not now new, but it has to be examined whether in North-East also the same concept will hold any good.

The North-Eastern states figure among the most backward states in the country. In the pre-independence period, the North-Eastern Region was a big rural un-industrialised region. Industrialisation itself was almost non-existent in N.E barring brisk activities in sectors like Oil and Tea etc. The forward and backward linkages adversely affected the N-E Region in those days. There was no scope either for ushering in industrialisation by outsiders or for growth of local entrepreneurs. Even now also private sector participation in industries is not high. The entrepreneur class has not yet developed in N-E. In this background the various states Govt. of the N-E have come up in a big way by setting up SLPE's for the all round development of these states. In context of the genesis, growth and inevitability of the SLPE's in the North-Eastern states some questions arise and need to be studied.

The objectives of the SLPE's in N-E differ from their counterparts—the validity of this hypothesis is to be tested. Whether the general disabilities that grow out of economic backwardness of the state in N-E like lack of industrial culture is compounding the situation in N-E? Should the PE's performing primarily for fulfilment of social objectives be adequately subsidised by the Govt. for losses suffered by them in fulfilment of these objectives? Whether and how to take hard decisions with regard to the closure, merger and privatisation of SLPE's in N-E How far privatisation would be successful in N-E? How to draw turn around plans/professionalisation of P.E cadres.

If we have to continue with the system of PE's detailed studies would be required in the following critical areas—those relating to institutional and policy framework; what should be the basic task and philosophies of an operating enterprise in N-E; what should be the design of the intervention processes fitting the abilities of the enterprises and other resources; what are the strengths, weaknesses, opportunities, potentials and threats of the PE's in N-E; how to develop the competitive spirit; those relating to the inter-relationship of Government & P.E; what should be the role of Govt. in promoting and developing, these enterprises; are the PE's generating meaningful employment. Is there excessive Govt. interference in day to day functioning.

Those relating to the PE's managerial process and organisational structure what should be the management techniques to suit the local conditions, how to manage the behavioural aspects of the enterprises. There has apparently been little systematic work under above aspects, the importance of which cannot be ever denied. The core problems, that we all should try to solve in the 1990s itself is how to prepare the new design for the SLPE's of N-E which would be suitable for 2000s and beyond.

12. SOCIAL CHANGE AND DEVELOPMENT AND EDUCATION

—Gauri Deka

Society is ever changing. One of the major factors for change is education. Education may be both formal and informal. With the tremendous increase in population in this region the institutions for education also have undergone changes in number as well as in the functions. It is necessary, therefore, to study with utmost priority the basic elements of human life and institutions in this (North-East) region. This would help in minimising the tension among the individuals and group which would eventually lead to evolve a suitable system of education which would have the innate characteristics of controlling the behaviour of the individual as well as that of the group and establishing their inter-relationship for the good of the humanity.

Education is related to every aspect of human life, so it is related to all other social sciences like Sociology, Anthropology, Economics, Political Science, etc. Most of the problems in education are related to different aspects of the life in the society. So all the studies can be taken as interdisciplinary studies. The field of research and investigation in education is vast; but here I would like to mention only a few areas where I deem priorities should be given.

Universalisation of Primary Education

The initiatives taken by the Government and the voluntary agencies, Primary Education in India has gained a momentum, but such studies as impact of education on children of the families where parents are illiterate, incidence of wastage and stagnation and education of parents, difficulties faced by first-generation learners at home and school, may be some of the areas for study.

Education and Constitutional Equality

The Constitution of India has given equality to all citizens of India but are the people who are so long been neglected or looked down upon enjoying this equality, if not then why, in which respect they are still remaining isolated or segregated from the larger section of the society. Question of reservation of seats in educational institutions may also be studied.

Women and Education

Several studies on women have considered the development of their social status and education. But, areas like their role and status in the rural areas, are rather few. The latter also includes themes like education of girls—in the changing situations parental opinions, ideas and attitudes toward—the preparation of their girl children for future (Their education, vocation, etc.). These are to be considered as research priorities and efforts should also include the need for understanding the girl students, their ambitions, aspirations, abilities, difficulties as well as the impact of the changing social situations.

Education and Economics

Economic conditions of the people is very much associated with education, for human resource development—Cost of education, Economic growth and education, Educational finance, National Planning and Educational Planning—are some of the areas where priorities may be given for study. Employment is closely related to education, the status, conditions, difficulties in this area required through probe, vocational education, vocationalisation of Secondary Curriculum—may also be included.

Culture and Education

Region comprises of various population groups with their own culture—Patterns of indigenous education of different groups, the impact of modern education on such cultures, trends of westernisation in such cultures, may be considered.

Education and Youths

In the changing scenario of the societies in this region, several very serious problems have arisen. Deeper studies in these areas may help in ameliorating such problems among these, insurgency in N-E Region, smoking alcoholism and drug addiction have taken a very serious and dangerous shape. Deeper studies should be carried on in this field, criminality and youths—increasing incidence of violence, theft, robbery, cheating where students are gradually getting involved into also require proper study.

A group of youths have also started standing against the social evils, malpractices and superstitions etc. Student activism in this region—its impact of such actions on socio-political life of the people may also be considered.

Education and Health

Education aims at developing a healthy mind in a healthy body. To do this a well organised health care service should be developed which may render care starting from the expecting mother continuing through the years of development of children may offer several areas for study, only a few may be mentioned here such as availability and acceptance of health care services, anomalies in field of physical growth, physical as well as mental care of adolescents—guidance services etc. may be probed into—better and deeper consideration in this respect may, bring up many more areas. My attempt is only to point out to some areas where necessity of probing into is felt.

13. COMBATING DRUG MENACE

—D.N. Barthakur

Earlier studies were not concerned with regard to the vices of drug abuse though alcoholism was very popular in the region as because most of the tribal communities of the region have been customarily using alcohol. It has been observed that alcohol finds inroad even into the non-tribal societies where it was previously prohibited. Most of the youths gradually have become victims of drug. These youths are our own fellowmen and they are the future generation of the country. It is very pitiable that this future generation is in the grip of drug abuse and alcoholism. This devastating vice has changed the ethnological aspects of the society in general and the addicts in particular by debilitating them psychologically as well as physically. Also, this abuse, plays a significant role in deteriorating further generations since children born of addicts may be physically handicapped. Drug abuse and alcoholism not only cause personal disaster of the addicts but also adversely affect the socio-economic system. As such the prime need of the social scientists today is to work out the strategy for prevention of drug abuse and alcoholism in order to eradicate the evil practices and to save the young generation from the clutches of the great demon of drug abuse and alcoholism. But how it can be done? It is in this context priority should be given for undertaking research on this area. This broad area may again be divided into sub-themes such as:

1. Problems of drug abuse and alcoholism;
2. Socio-economic aspects of drug abuse and alcoholism;
3. Medical counselling to drug abuse and alcohol addicts;
4. Problem of Rehabilitation of the drug & alcohol addicts;
5. Remedial measures.

14. WOMEN UNDER ENACTED LEGISLATIONS

—Jeuti Barooah

Reliance on law is one of the main characteristics of modern society to bring about social change. But legislation in our country enacted so far is out of reach for most women. Because, they have neither the mental awareness nor the financial resources to take advantage of the beneficiary provisions of legislations. Like other parts of the country, in North-Eastern Region too, the women are not getting adequate opportunity to exercise their legal rights and freedom in the society. They are socially and economically not capable of reaping the benefits of law. This will be evident if we examine the provisions of some important legislations relating to women mainly in the spheres of matrimonial laws, maintenance, succession etc. Generally our women are shy about going to the court for any relief under the provisions of the Acts, e.g. the Hindu Marriage Act which provides for divorce and prohibits bigamy. Marriage confers on a husband the legal obligation to maintain his wife provided she is chaste and unable to maintain herself.

Maintenance under Sec. 125 of the Cr. P.C. legislation of Hindu-Women Property rights and Succession Act, 1937 etc. are some of the important legislations. But our women are still ignorant of these provisions. Because of the financial difficulties, lack of awareness and assistance from her kin, a widow has often to forego her share of husband's property. There has been a change through the provisions of the Hindu Succession Act, 1956, whereby daughters and the widows of the deceased can also inherit shares equal to those of the sons. Property laws have been greatly modernised to provide legal share to a woman. However, the force of custom still dominates laws.

In the tribal areas of the North-Eastern Region, where the customary laws and practices are prevailing, the different tribal communities are in a state of flux. The womenfolk of these societies are experiencing myriad problems of adjustments. A tribal woman of N-E Region is exactly the same as any other woman of the country with the same passions, love and fear, the same devotion to the home, to husband and children, the same faults and the same virtues. Where the tribal woman differs from her more sophisticated sisters is in the kind of life she lives and her position in society almost without any protection of law.

To take only one or two examples, polygamous marriage as allowed by customary laws in Arunachal Pradesh and Manipur has given rise to difficult problems for married women. The system of bride price has also created complicated problems. Her legal status is varied again both in the matrilineal and patrilineal societies in respect of property and family affairs. It needs a comprehensive study to ascertain the legal status of women in N-E Region, comprising all the states.

In the present day society violence against women is manifested in several forms. It includes rape, demands for dowry, mental and physical cruelty harassment to the point where suicide becomes the only means of escape for a woman. The victim still lives under the social stigma and will have to pay a high price for reporting the rape case. Legal protection relating to the incident of rape on woman under the provision of I.P.C. is also an important aspect to be studied.

Another important legislation is the Immoral Traffic (Prevention) Act, 1956 amended in 1986. There are provisions under Sec. 5 for punishment in the said Act for procuring, inducing or taking woman or girl for the sake of prostitution. It also provides the punishment (U/S 6) for detaining a woman or girl in premises where prostitution is carried on, for (Sec. 8) seducing or soliciting for purpose of prostitution etc. Thus there are various beneficent legal provisions to safeguard a woman which may assist her to assert her rights. Besides, there are other legislations like (1) Dowry Prohibition Act, 1961, (2) the Medical Termination of Pregnancy Act, 1971, (3) Equal Remuneration Act, 1976, (4) the Family Courts Act, 1984 etc., to safeguard women against social and moral exploitation. But it can safely be stated that the implication of these legislations are yet to be effective in our society. Due to lack of publicity and propaganda, there may not be any impact of these provisions among the women of this N-E Region.

Social legislation could become effective only when there is organised voluntary effort to make the people understand the values of these statutory laws. It is not enough unless an environment is created for implementation of these legal provisions. We must create awareness among the people by active participation in this regard.

15. RESEARCH IN WOMEN'S STUDIES

—Mrs. S.L. Baruah

1. Women Studies

This is a virgin field of study in North-East India. Till date research on this area is confined to women's social status and their role in the freedom struggle, and that too, to the non-tribal or Hindu women in the main. No systematic study on the tribal women in this region has yet been taken up. However, in view of the emerging women's movements and organisations in North-East India and also of the reports on the atrocities on women by family and state agencies, the following areas may be suggested for research.

a) Women's Movements in North-East India

It will study the nature of women's movements in the region; aims, objectives and composition of different women organisations in the North-East, both professional and non-professional on local, state and regional level; their pattern and dimension of activities; their plans and programmes for women, children and social welfare (like rehabilitation of destitute women and children, establishment of pre-primary school, removal of illiteracy, supply of drinking water, proper service in the primary health centres, imparting training on certain vocations, etc.); their inter-relationship and link with women organisations of the national level. It will also study the extent of their success in carrying out their plans and programmes, obstacles hindering their development and suggest measures for improvement of the present situation. A comparative study of professional and non-professional, rural and urban or between leading women organisations of different states of the North-East would perhaps be more useful and fascinating.

b) Atrocities on Women

This may also be titled as Violence on Women or as Crime against Women. It will study both physical and psychological/emotional violence committed on women by family, society and state. Cases of rape, molestation, wife-beating, murder of women etc., are increasing day by day in this region, particularly in the states of Assam and Tripura. The study will investigate such cases with a view to finding out the social position of both the victim and the culprit, the role of the police, physician, court, administration, political leaders, intellectuals and women organisations—impact of different forms of violence on the health and morale of the victim, attitude of the family and the society towards such women—services rendered by the rescue homes or District Welfare Departments etc. The study will suggest ways and means to stop crime against women. Different interview schedules will have to be prepared for interviewing the victim, the culprit and the personnel and authorities associated with it.

c) Girl Child

It will study gender disparity in both traditional and modern, backward and advanced/educated families. A comparative study of the attitude towards the girl child in rural and urban families will facilitate a comprehensive idea of the problem. The study will cover within its perimeter education and health of the girl child, her engagement in and outside the family and the opportunities enjoyed by her to develop her personality. It will bring out statistical findings of female drop outs in different schools, ratio between boys and girls prosecuting higher education, number of girl labourers in the tea gardens and different industries as wage earners and as domestic servants in a given area—their right to their income, their mental up-bringing their consciousness of the self, their world view, their attitude towards marriage, their concern about their future etc.

Leaving aside these three thrust areas studies may also be undertaken on problem like Women and Health, Women and Environment, Women and Science and Technology, Women and Development, Crime Amongst Women etc.

2. Tribal Studies

So far social change among different tribes of the North-East region and their history and culture only are being studied and that too taking each tribe in isolation. A comprehensive study of their religious and cultural ethos and their social institutions and inter-tribal economic and political relations have not yet been taken up. Impact of modernisation on tribal situation in North-East India, tribal development and such problems may also be studied. A comparative study of ethnic awareness and autonomy movements between different tribes of the region will facilitate a better understanding for the tribal problems and aspirations and give clue to their solutions.

16. RURAL-URBAN DICHOTOMY

—N.N. Bhattacharyya

'Rural-urban dichotomy' in development is one of the fundamental concerns of developing societies today. What is most disturbing is that dichotomy seems to increase as the development processes proceed further. The large urban centres have emerged as centres of high concentration of population, income and industrialisation. Against this, the economy of the rural areas has more or less remained stagnant. Large scale industries and large urban centres tended to siphon off skilled people from the rural areas and gradually resources too. Unequal terms of trade on the one hand and discordance between agriculture and manufacturing on the other became consequential and later causal factors of rural stagnation. This may be one of the thrust areas of geographical and social science research in N-E India.

17. ISSUES IN URBAN POVERTY

—P. Deka

Long and serious debates are going on about the methods of determining the magnitude of urban poverty, providing urban basic services and in moving total quality of life of the urban poor. The National Commission on Urbanisation observed that "....our attitude towards urban settlements has been somewhat confused. On one hand we see them as heroic engines of growth creating skills and wealth for nation and also generating employment for the waves of distress migrants from rural areas and on other hand we also see them as unavoidable places of many social and economic disparities."

There are serious disputes about the extent of urban poverty in the country. But the glaring facts remain that a substantially high proportion of urban population is still poor. However, poverty can not be characterised by the extent of absolute number of people whose consumption expenditure is below a particular officially determined level. The nature of urban poverty is compounded by proliferation of slums, lack of minimum basic needs like—shelter, drinking water supply, employment opportunities and other environmental sanitation facilities. The national commission on urbanisation observed that urban poverty is a multidimensional concept that includes access to services, social and psychological supports and environment. The commission further observed that the "household income concept of poverty" missed the environmental and shelter characteristics of the neighbourhood.

During the Sixth and Seventh Five Year Plans many income generating and neighbourhood development programmes have been evolved under the central sector. Gradually, due to financial constraints the responsibility of funding and implementation has been shifted to the states and local governments. As a result, more and more emphasis towards strategies like—public-private partnership, involvement of NGOs, community based participation, cost sharing in planning, implementation and also management has been given. Naturally, the role of the government from being the 'provider' has been shifted to becoming the 'facilitator'. In this situation, it has been increasingly felt that people's participation in the context of present day urban reality is no longer a liberal ideal; it is a compelling necessity.

Therefore, the problems of urban poverty, slums, basic services for the poor and urban environment are assuming great significance. It becomes increasingly important to develop a mechanism between the government and people's participation—both at organisational and individual level. This has helped the urban poor to improve the total quality of life. This appears to be the pivotal issue in urban poverty. The above issue leads to the identification of three major group of thrust areas for study. Magnitude of urban poverty; Theoretical perspectives regarding urban poverty; Prevalence of poverty among different social groups, Slum dwellers and such other considerations; Steps taken by the government for improving the condition of the urban poor; Effectiveness of the programmes including monitoring; Institutional set-up at state as well as local government levels; Development of a centralised data-base through local level case studies.

Nature and Extent of People's Participation including the study of Decentralised planning process and its effectiveness. Present nature of participation at individual, family and community level including NGOs. Identification of factors in determining the success of participation services. Role of community participation as an instrument to improve quality of life of the urban poor. Sustaining activities—Development of linkages, Motivating people for participation, Development of skills for improving productivity. Women's participation in income generating activities. Creation of productive assets at individual and at community levels. Creation of community based common facility centres for training and production. It is felt that improvement of quality of life of the urban poor will be possible only when the issues relating to urban poverty, basic services and people's participation have been understood clearly, analysed critically and developed a workable mechanism for implementation of various urban poverty alleviation programmes. This will be possible through extensive field studies conducted specially in the thrust areas mentioned above.

URBAN STUDIES IN HISTORICAL PERSPECTIVES

In historical study of North-East India, this aspect of the subject has not yet received due attention. Although some works have been done in this field in allied disciplines and a few in history as well. There is scope for urban studies relating to each of the industrial and capital towns and those having historical importance like those of Sibsagar, Lakhimpur, Sadiya, Dimapur, Imphal. Planned archaeological excavations have not yet been taken up in any place of the North-East region and many spots still remain unidentified or outside the pale of history. This can also be investigated. Study on urbanisation in Assam with a view to bringing out the different stages of urbanisation and the link of the urban centres of this region with those of India and neighbouring countries like Tibet and China in ancient and medieval times is expected to bring to light new facts relating to the history and culture of this region.

Extent of urbanisation, its impact on the socio-economic life of the people including demographic pattern promoting both integrating and disintegrating forces, impact of urbanisation on environment and ecology etc. are important aspects to be covered within urban studies.

IMPACT OF URBANISATION ON FAMILY AND KINSHIP

Due to the impact of urban industrial growth, the social situation in Assam has undergone significant changes.

Urbanisation has produced a two-fold impact on the family and kinship system of Assamese society :It has provided new opportunities for education and employment in the society and, it has provided the scope for break up of the joint family system weakening the kinship organisation.

Consequential Effects of the Above Mentioned Change and Developments

The educational and occupational opportunities have contributed to the emergence of working parents. The new phenomenon of single mothers is also a remarkable consequence of such opportunities. On the other hand, the weakening of the kinship organisation has undermined the kinship help and cooperation available to every individual. The break up of the joint family system has produced an insecure environment to the old parents. Assessment of adjustment to changes in family life is required to be studied to analyse; Parental dependency, Relationships with grand children, Adjustment problems for Men and Women, Adjustment to singlehood, Living arrangements etc.

The traditional security is diminished in the nuclear family system, especially in a denuded nuclear family. In an urban setting, it has become a problem for the working parents to provide association, attention and care to their children by carrying the responsibilities of parenthood. Consequently, the children are deprived of acquiring the preliminary socialising experiences. The most important forms of social behaviour necessary for successful social adjustment appear and begin to develop at this time in the early years of childhood. Lack of attachment with the working parents has enhanced the freedom and independence to children and adolescence, increased their decision making power and enabled them to judge the traditional customs and behaviour. In attempting to adjust themselves in a new situation, they have been forced by circumstances to seize the newly opened opportunities for substitute companions. Adolescents want as friends those whose interests and values are similar to theirs, who understand them and make them feel secure and in whom they can confide problems and discuss which they cannot share with their parents. Young children are impulsive. They act without thinking. They respond to immediate stimuli without considering future consequences.

Violation of Social Norms

Every adolescent sooner or later discovers that money is the key to independence. Interest in money becomes an important element in independence. This interest centres mainly on how to earn easy money, regardless of the kind of work done. As a result crimes committed by juveniles are increasing day by day which included those under the Indian Penal Code and the Local and Special laws. Disharmony, conflict, non-conformity, occasional violence of social norms are easily observable in a family of an urban setting. Violation of the social norm leads to social anomaly. Social scientists may try to find out some socio-cultural mechanism for the maintenance of equilibrium, social order, tranquillity and peace among the members composing the unit.

Education

Difficult on either linguistic or cultural basis, there will be few benefits as far gaining proficiency in the language is concerned (Vincent & Carter: 1986: 214). Learners as Akyel and Yelci (1990: 174–179), Pathak (1988) and others found have certain expectations from a syllabus, an expectation in terms of attaining ability in certain skills. When a syllabus fails in equipping the learners with those skills there is frustration and no language learning takes place.

In the context of the north-east the problem one faces is that the syllabii make a statement regarding the books to be studied and the items of grammar to be learnt. The teacher in the classroom paraphrases the lessons and teaches the grammatical items with some illustrations in the form f isolated sentences. The main aim of language teaching is to develop ability in the real life situation language or to use Munby's phrase 'realia' (1968). His expect in the elite English medium schools does not happen. The reasons for better ability in English in these schools is perhaps due to the fact that their exposure to English is not limited to the English class alone, but they are exposed to the English during their other classes as well. This does not happen to the majority of the learners coming from the vernacular medium schools. Hence their competence in English is almost negligible. The primary priority in research in language teaching has thus to concentrate on this area. To find an approach which can take care of the lack of opportunities for exposure to 'realia' and yet develop reasonable proficiency in the language.

In the fifties Chomsky brought about a revolution in the field of Linguistics and Language Teaching through this transformative and generative approach to linguistics. He differentiated between 'competence' and 'performance' of a learner in a language. Competence he defined as the knowledge of the rules of language operation while 'performance' was the ability to use those rules in a real life situation. Chomsky felt that competence does not automatically lead to performance. This becomes the basis for a whole lot of theories coming up in the field of Language Teaching and a host of new approaches to Language Teaching being innovated and adapted in the last three decades. Wilkins in 1976 developed his famous National Syllabus which he later modified as the 'situational approach'. Wilkins felt that in order to develop proficiency one need to taught the language in terms of notified time, space, length etc., and these must be taught in a real life situation. Widdowson in 1978 brought out another important approach called 'the communicative approach' to language teaching. He introduced the two concepts of 'usage' and 'use' and the appropriateness of use in a particular context. According to him 'usage' was the grammatically accepted utterance, whereas 'use' was the acceptable utterance in a communicative situation. The real test of the proficiency in language came from the ability of learners to use the language appropriately in the given context. The emphasis in the communicative approach is thus on teaching the 'use' of the language rather than the 'usage'. It is in this context that the importance of the situational teaching and the creation of a communicative environment assumes its importance.

Like most parts of India the emphasis in the North-East is on the teaching of the usage in isolation and hence, problems in proficiency. The learners are often unable to transfer their knowledge about the rules of grammar to actual use. Quite often the rules are over generalised and peculiar use of the rules is to be observed. The researchers have therefore to concentrate on the actual situations in the classrooms in schools and colleges of the region and suggest modifications in the strategies of teaching learning so that the aspirations of the students and the needs of the society can be satisfied.

The other important area which needs priority is the development of the curriculum for language teaching. It must be accepted that the text book still remains the best available medium for language learning-teaching. Replacing the text-book with audio-visual aids or more intensive situational methods may not be practicable. The disastrous Bombay University reforms with the English syllabus, where the textbook was replaced by certain language skills to be taught by teacher not from any particular textbooks, has perhaps taught us that replacing the textbook may not be wise. In the Indian context a language teacher is to a great extent dependent on the text-book and takes away much of the confidence of the teacher. Hence, research on the contents of the textbook has to be undertaken in the context of the needs of language in the north-east.

In this context research has to be concentrated on two aspects. Firstly, the group of learners needs have to specifically predicted and then this specification can be used to determine the content of a language programme that will meet these needs. Thus, if, for example, we can specify what students of economics need to be able to do with English by analysing their textbooks or what waiters need to be able to do with English by analysing their interaction with patrons, we can device custom made courses of English that incorporate the results of the analysis (Widdowson 1984 : 177). The contention while framing a textbook for a language syllabus has essentially to be concentrated on as Munby observes, "The syllabus specification of the communication needs of that particular participant or community" (Munby 1978 : 218).

The most unfortunate part of curriculum planning in the north-east has been the fact that no research has preceded the language needs of the community. The aim of syllabus framers has been to fill in textbooks with poems, prose pieces and plays or grammatical items. The question of the amount of language learnt, or the type of language learnt has never language particularly English. Wilkins observes on the contents of a language syllabus:

> The process of deciding what to teach is based on considerations of what the learners should most usefully be able to communicate in the target language. The labelling for the learning units is not primarily semantic. A general language course will concern itself with those concepts and functions that are likely to be of widest value. In the provision of a course for a more specialised language learner the limitation is on the types of content he needs to express and not the number of structures he needs to know or the situations in which he will find himself. In short, the linguistic content is planned according to the semantic demands of the learner (Wilkins 1976: 19).

The learning units have to be redefined as "concepts and functions" rather than as structures. The learning units are themselves derivable from the desired terminal behaviour. Syllabus content must be determined by the goals rather than the process of learning. This research has first to identify the goals and then identify the process, which would be the priority of research in language teaching.

When a learner starts actually using a second language or a foreign language it is generally observed that some deviations from the rules of language operation takes. In Linguistics these deviations are classified as errors. In the traditional approaches as the learners inability to internalise the rules and thus errors always required some remedial measures like reinforcement and pattern practice to errors. It is now generally accepted that errors are a part and parcel of the process of language acquisition. They reflect a "transitional competence" of the learner in a language (Selinker, 1972). Besides the errors are also indicative of the problems being faced by the learners while trying to internalise the system of another language. This also helps in the evaluation of the efficiency of teaching-learning strategies being adopted for the teaching of a language. Thus "Error Analysis" has become an important area for the analysis of learning difficulties in a particular area.

It has been observed that sources of errors and patterns of errors vary from place to place and sometimes from individual to individual. This perhaps gave rise to the concept of "learner's idiolect" (Pit Corder 1967) and the fact that each learner needs a separate language curriculum. However, in a country like India and a region like the north-east this is not practicable and we have to think about activity. Research therefore, has to concentrate on the analysis of errors as reflective of two basic problems of the learners. The problems generated by the teaching-learning system as a whole, like emphasis on the unimportant aspects of cases it has been observed that interference from the mother-tongue also causes errors. Research in Mizoram shows that interference from the mother tongue is responsible for about 20 percent of the errors. Research is needed in this area to evaluate the number, area and significance of the errors for better understanding of the problems of teaching-learning.

It has been observed that the curriculum of teaching-learning has to reflect the aspirations and needs of learners and society alike. Language syllabii, particularly syllabii of English seem to show the widest gap between the aspirations and what is actually received from them. The problems emanate from a variety of reasons like inappropriate methodology of teaching, inadequate material of teaching and improper approaches to testing and valuations. Remedial measures have in most of the cases been on an ad-hoc basis without research into the backgrounds needs and aspirations. In a remote place like the north-east the priorities of research have thus to be in these areas connected with the teaching of English and other languages. Most of the research in this area has been concentrated on the literatures of the languages and now these priorities should change.

CHAPTER 2

The Barak Valley

This chapter deals with basic issues relating to the Barak Valley. Barak Valley has got a distinct geographical identity. It is a part of the State of Assam but has no similarity in respect of language, culture tradition even culture orientation. Barak Valley was part of the mainland now called Bangladesh. British made a single geographical entity mainly for political convenience and viability. Ever since Barak Valley became a part of the State of Assam there was social tension, political and economic discrimination. Mentally the people of the Valley never expressed their identification with the other valley. In the state, the economic, social and political development, has been frequently interpreted as a result of the bias of the majority community. There is thus a probability that it may lead to alienation of other distinct population groups in the state. Let us look at the economic development of the State of Assam then we will be able to generalise the condition of Barak Valley. Barak Valley has got vast tea, minerals, water, forest, agriculture potentials but the proverb goes that it lives on money order. There is all-round degeneration and deceleration.

As a result, some groups are demanding separation, some are demanding a Union Territory status, some are demanding autonomy, and so on. Rigid attitudes and extreme ideologies led to armed struggle. Yet, there are instances like the movements for autonomy that paved way to armed struggle highlighting alienation and frustration among the population groups in the Barak Valley.

The panelists agreed that in the coming decade peoples' concern over identity and demand for political autonomy, for

Barak Valley was going to be a major issue in political arena. Consequently, discussions were focussed on the extent of popular acceptance of the demand for autonomy in the context of Barak Valley, its justification, and viability of the said proposal.

It is to be admitted at the very outset that the North-East India does not manifest a homogenous identity. Not only its components different from each other, but also cleavage, diversity and contradiction exist within a single political unit. Thus it is hardly possible to thrash out enough academic exercises, a set of common priorities that would suit the entire region. This simple fact deserves to be considered while identifying the research priorities of the Barak Valley. Administratively the valley is an integral part of Assam, but its priorities cannot be equated with that of the Brahmaputra Valley since the differences that exist between the two valleys are basic in some major aspects.

The form and contest of their differences can as well be framed into a research hypothesis but since the social science research of the present day demands a more purposeful approach, we are inclined to suggest that the practical manifestation of this difference which has already developed into a contradiction between the valleys offers us a more meaningful areas of study. We feel that a study of the contradiction that exist between the Brahmaputra Valley and the Barak Valley should come first while identifying the research priorities of the Barak Valley. And to make this study effective and result oriented, an investigation into the functioning of the state power since independence vis-a-vis the Barak Valley can be undertaken.

The objective of such an effort is to examine the validity of the popular perceptions prevalent in the Barak valley—of discrimination and deprivation by the Brahmaputra Valley and the partisan attitude of the state power. This widely prevalent notion has never been examined though this notion plays a dominant role in determining the issues of public importance in the Barak valley.

To make the study convincing it will be necessary to make a comparative assessment of the two valleys with regard to achievements in the priority sectors of the economy. The cultural aspect of the problem is essentially linked with the language policy pursued by the state power, Special emphasis is due on seeking on answer to two basic questions: (a) whether the language policy of the state has an expansionist character and (b) whether the language has become vehicle of oppression and deprivation on the zones inhabited by linguistic minorities. Concern over identity and demand for political autonomy were the two related questions of both the Barak Valley and the Brahmaputra Valley. In both areas destabilising factors have come to dominate. The discussions also suggested the irrelevance of the national political parties who had not only failed to identify themselves with people's hopes and aspirations but also could not pay due regard to peoples concern over identity, as a result of which, people's demand was now emerging from the grass roots. Besides, it was also felt that granting of political autonomy alone was not enough to provide answer to the multifarious problems faced by the people and the different regions, even after gaining autonomous status, continued to show restlessness and difference among themselves. So that the question of viability bore little relevance.

Thus the issues concerning the Barak Valley that needs a comprehensive study, includes:

Section I: Economic and Social History of Barak Valley

i) Pre-colonial history of Barak Valley.
ii) Economic history of Barak Valley, particularly, from the early to the British period.
iii) Impact of Vaishavion on the religious and socio-cultural integration in North-East India.
iv) Analysis and documents of folk literature of Barak Valley.

Section II: Economics

i) Inter-district disparities in economic development with reference to the share of different districts in governments plan and non-plan outlay.
ii) Productive relations in agriculture in Barak Valley and the impact of such relations on agricultural growth.

iii) Economic Development and the dynamics of class-formation in Barak Valley.
iv) Problems of Capital-formation in North-East India: Nature of accumulation and re-investment of surplus.
v) Tea Industry in Barak Valley—study of productivity, cost effectiveness ownership pattern, labour relations, extraction and re-investment of surplus.
vi) Industrialisation Strategy and the states, particularly, strategy of the role of the state-level public sector undertakings and the District Industries Centres.
vii) Nature of implementation of DRDA, NREP and Tribal Area Development Programmes: Case Studies at village level.
viii) Management of Infrastructure (particularly power, transport and communication): Survey of the problems and the potentialities for developing alternative modes.
ix) Technology and Development: Studies suggesting alternative and appropriate technologies for North-East India.

Section III: Political Science, Sociology and Environment

i) Study of the different ethnic and linguistic groups, particularly focusing on the elements of continuity and change in their patterns of livelihood and their reaction and response towards the emerging political and economic order.
ii) Electoral politics and voting behaviour in Barak Valley.
iii) Peoples participation in the decision-making process: Survey of the nature and functioning of the Panchayats and co-operative societies in Barak Valley.
iv) Problems of the linguistic, religious and ethnic minorities in North-East India and the role of state legislatures in the protection of their rights.
v) Identify question, the medium issue and the language movements in Barak Valley.
vi) Demand for Autonomy in Barak Valley and in other parts of North-East India: Study of the background, genesis and also the rulers response to such popular demands.
vii) Labour Problems and Trade-Unionism in Barak Valley.
viii) Women studies, particularly focusing upon the participation of women-labour in the industries, in agriculture and

in other productive sectors, and on the elements of continuity and change in the status of women in this region.

ix) Studies on the nature and impact of deforestation.

x) Problems of education, with particular reference to Adult-literacy.

Section IV

i) The Identity Question in Barak Valley in the context of the valley being a Bengali majority area in a so-called Assamese majority state.

ii) Status of Bengali language in Assam and its problems.

iii) Biography of illustrations of Barak Valley.

iv) Study of the different ethnic groups of Barak Valley.

v) History of Barak Valley.

vi) The socio-political and cultural impact of migration upon the Barak valley society.

vii) The socio-political as well as the economic background of communal misunderstanding now being observed in Barak Valley.

viii) State and the people of Barak valley, particularly the latters alienation, problems and grievances.

ix) Studies exploring the economic potentialities of Barak Valley.

Section V

i) The people and society in Barak Valley and the areas of their unity and contradictions;

ii) Concern of the people in Barak Valley over identity, their reaction and response;

iii) Analysis of peoples political behaviour, the language movements and other political movements in Barak Valley.

iv) Impact of the international border with Bangladesh, particularly the cultural, social and emotional effects of Bangladesh over the life of the people of the valley.

Section VI: The roots and historical process of emergence of Barak Valley's society

i) Study of village formation in Barak Valley, and

ii) Study of the process of transition of society in Barak Valley from a rural and agrarian framework to a semi-urban and non-agrarian set-up, and the socio-economic impact of such transition.

iii) the importance of manuscript study for gaining a better understanding of the history of early and medieval Cachar and the collection, and particularly, the cataloguing of historically relevant manuscripts.

iv) the democratic institutions and the democratic form of protests, in Barak Valley, the resultant alienation of the people giving rise to their feeling of deprivation and its ultimate culmination into the demand for autonomous political status for the valley, in terms of economic, cultural and political aspects.

v) Study of the co-operative movement in Barak Valley and of the causes of failure of the movement; Studies regarding the character of political protests; Municipal administration, its gradual disintegration in this region.

vi) History of the labour movement in Barak Valley, particularly in the valley's tea industry.

vii) Economic stagnation, the decline in economic growth and analysis of the factors contributing towards the fall in real per capita income; land tenure system, farm holding size and productive relations in agriculture; Survey of resource potential.

viii) Identity question and the background of autonomy movement in Barak Valley.

ix) Survey of economic resources and prospects of economic growth in Barak Valley; Problems of transport and liability of alternative modes of transport; Problems and prospects of power generation; The Socio-economic impact of the international border with Bangladesh; and plan allocations and the nature of utilisation.

x) Problems of primary and middle level education in Barak Valley and extent of societal participation in building up the educational infrastructure.

xi) human rights situation in Barak Valley.

CHAPTER 3

Recommendations

RESEARCH PRIORITIES IN ASSAM

Introduction

The Institute of Social Change and Development (ISCD) organised a local level Panel Discussion on Research Priorities in North-East. The Panel Discussion was sponsored by the North Eastern Regional Centre (Shillong) of the Indian Council of Social Science Research (ICSSR-NERC). It was one of the series of panel discussions sponsored by the NERC-ICSSR for different states in the region.

The objective of the Panel Discussion was to identify priority areas where discipline-specific as well as inter-disciplinary Social Science Research were needed for speedier social, cultural and economic development of the region. The identification of the thrust areas, it was hoped, would help in proper utilisation of scarce resource and at the same time make social science research relevant to the regional needs. The ISCD invited some 60 scholars and social workers belonging to the various academic, research institutes and other organisations located in Guwahati. These were also presented in the Panel Discussion.

The Panel Discussion was organised in 3 sessions. Dr. M. Taher and Dr. P.C. Goswami, members of the Governing Body of the ISCD acted as the co-ordinators in the sessions. The two co-ordinators summed up the deliberations in the concluding Session-III. Dr. A.C. Bhagabati, explained the objectives of the Panel Discussion.

Identification of Priority Areas and Topics of Research

The presentations were lively, and identified an impressive tally of 120 research areas and topics that required social science research inputs in the north-eastern region.

Research Orientation—Issues in Culture and Society in the North-East

Detailed study of tribal-non-tribal continua. Need to adapt research models to ground realities. A more balanced approach towards tradition-modernity distinction needed in the region. Need to conceive alternative models of development which are in tune with the traditional egalitarian outlook prevalent in the north-eastern societies. Study of traditional value systems, which are breaking down due to the onslaught of modernisation. Meaning of values as an area of research at structural level. Strengthening of analytical research, at different from colonial monographic studies of communities, as well as methodology in the light of critical theory. This, as a basis for developing a cultural theory for the region. Study of folklores and perceptions: folk science as a system of management of environment, economics and medicine. Study of indigenous systems of self-management. Study of cultural ecology from the indigenous viewpoint. The indigenous vision of environment and comprehension of how people have worked out ways to cope with environmental problems in various eco-community settings in the north-east.

A. The Ethnic Situation in the North-East

The problems of immigration, ethnic diversity and inter-ethnic relations in different State settings.

Ethnicity and violence—causes and consequences—need for ground situation studies in different locales to understand the emergence of violence in traditionally non-violent societies.

Geo-economic study of the problems and prospects of the area under Bodoland Autonomous Council. A thorough demographic and socio-economic study involving:

- Geographical basis
- Population pattern
- Resource base and resource utilisation
- People's perception, aspirations and prospective development measures

B. Women-centred Issues

- Sociological analysis of enacted laws pertaining to women.
- Assessment of opportunities for women to exercise their legal rights and freedom.
- Action research pertaining to implementation of legal provisions.
- Study of violence against women.
- Issues pertaining to women.
- Problems emanating from universalisation of primary education.

Problems of Education of first generation learners.

- Impact of education of children on the families where parents are illiterate.
- Incidence of wastage and stagnation.
- Examination of the gap between equality granted by the constitution and educational opportunities enjoyed by different sections of the regional populations.
- Problems of education among women, particularly in the rural areas. Assessment of specific difficulties.
- The economics of education—educational finance national planning and educational planning; education and employment; vocationalisation of education.
- The inter-face between modern education and indigenous cultures and societies:
  - Patterns of indigenous systems of education.
  - The impact of modern education on traditional societies and cultures.
  - Trends of modernisation and westernisation.
  - Social problems and the youths:
  - Insurgency in the N-E region
  - Drug addiction and alcoholism
  - Youth and criminality

- Student activism against social evils.
- Issues in land and agriculture.

Empirical study of the loss of land, real and perceived, suffered by the Assamese peasantry. Studies covering small areas—say at block levels to identify:

- Loss of land traditionally viewed as belonging to the whole community (common property resource) under the impact of colonialism.
- Loss of land to more productive peasants, either through sale or because of indebtedness, or due to simple land grabbing (Inter-community and inter-class land alienation in Assam).
- Loss of land in a presently immigrant dominated area which was once undoubtedly inhabited by the Assamese peasantry.
- Loss of land in a mixed area, preferably close to an urban area.

Tracing over a period of fifty years or so in two segments, pre-Independence and post-Independence, the actual transfer of land from X to Y to Z, and so on, with a view to establishing the nature of the deals, the broad identity of sellers/buyers/ grabbers/victims and thus present a broad pattern of the change in the ownership of agricultural land, and the changing agrarian relations in the state.

Small holders farming property syndrome in Assam identification poverty-stricken families by using land-holding size as criterion to throw light on the rural poor to find out solutions to their problems.

- Study of agricultural manpower—the missing link in agricultural development and planning.
- Transformation patterns of shifting cultivation in the hill areas.
- Impact of rural emigration on agricultural production.
- Role of horticulture in the economy of the rural people.
- Impact to agricultural marketing and transport on agricultural efficiency.
- Evaluation of the impact of irrigational command areas on agricultural productivity.

- Exploration of poultry-farming and pisiculture as profitable alternative to small-scale farming.
- Role of small-scale agro-based industries on rural economy.
- Impact of modern inputs on agricultural production and development.
- Empirical study of the land laws of indigenous peasantry.
- Agricultural performance on different spatial and cultural contexts of Assam.
- Land use study in the urban and peri-urban areas.
- Agricultural practices in the flood plain, built-up areas, foot hills (the hills-plains fringe) and high plain areas.

C. *The role and impact of rabi* crop cultivation on the life and living of immigrants in the charlands of Assam.

- Study of eco-farming practices in the char areas of Assam.
- Role of the periodic markets, especially in the physico-cultural contact zones.

Environmental Issues and Ecology

- Impact of industrial pollution on agriculture.
- Agricultural land use and ecological degradation—the nature and extent of horizontal expansion of agricultural land use encroaching into the wetlands, grazing fields, reserved forests and hill slopes.
- Depletion and degradation of forest areas leading to marginalisation of the socio-economic base of the tribal population.
- Generation of data base on ethnic-cultural perception on indigenous resources—identification of community lands, common property rights, sacred groves, etc.
- Implications of development efforts on various resource use and resource productions. Also, the linkages between various sectors, namely forestry, agriculture and livestock.
- Policy research in identified areas like environmental protection, health, women, etc. Examination of distributional effects of Governmental programmes at local and regional levels.
- Hazard mitigation studies in respect to flood, earthquake, landslide and soil erosion.

- Loss of agricultural productivity due to soil degradation and natural disaster.
- Displacement and dislocation of population due to proposed development projects like, flood control/irrigation, power, industry, etc. in the North East region.
- Impact studies in relation to development projects including wetlands and wastelands.
- Environmental studies of the urban areas: health, sanitation, housing, etc.
- Monitoring degradation of urban development physical and cultural.
- Rural women and environmental quality.
- Pattern of energy use (cooking & lighting) in rural areas.
- Problems of fuelwood in urban as well as in rural areas.
- Assessment of non-conventional energy programmes, e.g., bio-gas, solar, etc.

Issues in Urban Studies in the North-East

- Role of history in shaping the character of urban centres.
- The network of relations between rural and urban inhabitants in Assam and the on-going rural and urban link.
- Quality and content of socio-cultural life of recent rural migrants to urban centres; transportation of rural traditions.
- Nature and function of kinship and family in urban settings.
- Impact of urbanisation of family and kinship—emergence of disharmonious family organisation and problems like juvenile delinquency, drug addiction, immoral traffic in women, divorce, separation, etc.
- Study of children and youth behaviour in the context of urbanisation and changed parent-child relationship.

The Study of Rural-Urban Dichotomy

The consequence of siphoning-off of labour and skilled people by industries .and urban centres and discordance between agriculture and manufacturing as casual factors of rural stagnation.

The Impact of Urban Centres on Rural Areas

- Issues in urban poverty.
- Magnitude of urban poverty—theoretical perspectives; measure of poverty among different social groups; Governmental steps for improving the condition of the urban poor; development of a centralised data-base through local level case studies.
- Nature and extent of people's participation in poverty alleviation and welfare programmes for the urban poor.

The Study of the Informal Sector

- Identification of linkages between formal and informal sectors—critical issues would be to identify the activities undertaken by individuals, households and work communities.
- Linkages and interdependence between the urban informal sectors and the rural informal sectors—primarily through seasonal, temporary and permanent migration and through the use of raw materials, recycling, use of by-products and small manufactures in home based units.
- Investigation of unrecovered urban economic activities find out the types of employment and activities and their roles in the urban socio-economic context.
- Study of women and the informal sector—the visible and the invisible role of women.
- The relationship between city size and informal sector.
- Detailed study of the concentration of informal sector activities in different spatial settings—rural, small town and city; distinctive activities, employment potential and cultural parameters.

Research areas in health, family welfare, mental health, nutrition, demography and cultural biology.

- Identification of linkages between socio-economic background and health status in various community settings in the following spheres:
- Survey of housing, water supply and sanitation standards—the gap between existing conditions and minimum required levels of development in these spheres in different regions.

- Study of traditional ideas, beliefs and practices connected with health and medicine.
- Base-line study of pollution level affecting health due to specific types of industrial activities in the north-east; for example, the high incidence of goitre among tea garden workers needs to be examined in this frame-work.
- Realistic assessment of family welfare programme and the socio-cultural constraints.
- Study of emerging, but burning problems like, AIDS, drug addiction and road accidents. The nexus between increasing drug-addiction/alcohol consumption and road accidents.
- Research aiming at the formulation of a realistic health education scheme.
- Study of the nature of perception and understanding about mental illness and attitude towards the mentally ill patients in different societies. This will help in developing programmes for the removal of superstition and stigma connected with mental illness.
- Assessment and evaluation of psychological stress factors, depressive illness and schizophrenia in the north eastern region in various community/social settings.
- Women and psychiatric problems. Study of incidence, societal attitudes, social stigma suffered by women because of it.
- Emergence of certain types of psychiatric syndrom in Assam while it is passing through a phase of social-political-demographic changes. Studies in different age-groups and social segments with a view to identify the linkage between psychological attributes (uncertainty, fear, anxiety, frustration, mistrust, paranoia) and social change.
- The psycho-social parameters of drug-addiction incidence, types of drug abuse, age-group and psycho-social stressors. Finding out the specific pattern which may be characteristic of this region.

Studies Relating to Geriatric Problems

Evaluation of the problems of the increasing numbers of aged persons in the context of changing socio-economic circumstances including family and kinship norms, in various societal settings of the north-east.

Studies Relating to Health and Nutrition

- Levels of malnutrition among different communities in the north-east in the context of varying ecological, ethnic, socio-economic and cultural conditions.
- Survey of physical growth and nutritional status among different population groups.

Studies Relating to Bio-demography

- Demographic response to changes in physical, biotic and social environment. Effect of cultural factors on fertility, mortality, morbidity and migration.
- Investigation into the changing demographic pattern of north eastern region in general and Assam in particular: study of socio-cultural imbalances caused by in-migration.
- Issues in regional economy, trade, industry, development and social change.

Resource Potentials and their Identification

- Assessment of the varied resources of the region—land, water, mineral, forest, etc. Preparation of inventories of resources as a basis for proper resource utilisation and maintenance of ecological balance.
- Critical assessment of infra-structural facilities (power, transport, irrigation, banking and financial institutions, etc.) at micro and macro levels.

Problems of Unemployment and Under-employment and Manpower Planning

- Extent, causes, types and socio-economic impact of the incidence of unemployment and under-employment.
- Manpower planning research with emphasis on demand and supply sides.

Problems of Poverty and Social Justice

- Nature and extent of poverty in rural and urban areas; causes of progressive pauperisation.
- Critical evaluation of the specific programmes of poverty and unemployment eradication like minimum needs programme, 20-point programme, IRDP, SFDA, NREP and its present version JRY, etc. Assessment of the qualitative impact of these programmes.
- Planning and development strategies—a critical assessment of the policies followed so far covering perspective planning, input-output tables, decentralised and micro-level planning, Panchayati Raj and people's participation at the grass-root level.
- Study of economic inter-dependence among various units of N-E India and the need for coordinated economic development of the region. Study of economic structure of various states of the region in an inter-regional framework.
- Identification of priority sectors of the region based on inter-sectoral linkages.
- Analysis of the role of North Eastern Council as an agent of balanced regional development.
- In-depth research on the working and performance of the public sector enterprise, including the sick state level ones (like, ASTC and ASEB) and also to consider the justification of privatisation of State Level Public Enterprises (SLPE).
- To examine the scope and preparation of a new design for the SLPEs. Since the motives for the establishment and existence of PEs are socio-economically conditioned, there performance cannot be measured with the same criterion as private enterprises. These must be measured not only in terms of financial profitability but also on the basis of their contribution to the general well-being of the society as a whole and other aspects of performance.

In the context of the genesis, growth and inevitability of the SLPEs in the North Eastern States, some questions that arise need to be stated:

The objectives of the SLPEs in N-E differ from their counterparts—the validity of this hypothesis is to be tested.

Whether the general disabilities that grow out of economic backwardness of the state in N-E like lack of industrial culture is compounding the situation in N-E?

Should the PEs performing priority for fulfilment of social objectives be adequately subsidised by the government for losses suffered by them in fulfilment of these objectives?

Whether and how to take hard decisions with regard to the closure, merger and privatisation of SLPEs in N-E?

How far privatisation would be successful in N-E?

How to draw turnaround plans/professionalisation of PE cadres?

If we have to continue with the system of PEs, detailed studies would be required in the following critical areas. Those relating to institutional and policy framework.

What should be the basic task and philosophies of an operating entreprise in N-E?

What should be the design of the intervention processes fitting the abilities of the enterprises and other resources?

What are the strengths, weaknesses, opportunities potentials and threats of the PEs in N-E?

How to develop the competitive spirit?

Those relating to the interrelationship of government and P.E.

What should be the role of government in promoting and developing these enterprises?

Are the PEs generating meaningful employment?

Is there successive government interference in day-to-day functioning?

Those relating to the PEs managerial process and organisational structure.

What should be the management technique to suit the local conditions?

How to manage the behavioural aspects of the enterprises?

The socio-cultural framework of development—studies relating to attitudes, aspirations, work culture, leisure habits, values, leadership pattern, organisational ability, etc., of the people which have a bearing on development:

- Identification of various weaknesses of the people of N-E India which hinder self-sustained development.

- Identification of backward areas and preparation of socio-economic profiles and levels of development.
- Regional disparities in the development of transport network and feeder roads which serve as a basis for sustainable growth and development.
- A study of the public distribution system with a view to minimise the gap between the haves and have notes in urban and rural areas.
- Research needs in the Villages and Small Industry (VSI) sectors.
- Enquiries covering infrastructure, ancilliary development, aspects of management, promotional organisations and their role, programme of development of village and small industry sector and their impact, sickness in small industry sector, development of entrepreneurship including developing entrepreneurship among women.
- Impact of Industrial Estate Programme on the development of small industry in the state or specific regional context.
- Prospects for development of ancillary industries based on the requirements of large and medium scale industries for promoting first generation entrepreneurs.
- Examination of the prospects of horticulture and food preservation and processing industries (cold storage, fruit canning, vegetable processing) as part of the rural employment generation and development package.
- Examination of the prospects of introduction of crops like remi for augmenting the textile sector and also strengthening and modernising the existing textile sector like that of muga.
- Examination of the role of District Industries centres in promoting entrepreneurship in the VSI sector.

Capital Investment in Small Industry Sector

- Evaluation of public expenditure and its impact on the economic development of Assam.
- Measurement of Government revenue and its administration in Assam: Different sources of government revenue, scope of increasing tax and non-tax revenues, problem of collection of revenue and its administration.

- An economic analysis of public enterprises—a break even analysis covering variable and fixed components of costs.
- Performance appraisal of public transport systems (ASTC and others) in Assam.
- Cost benefit analysis of poverty alleviation programme.
- Status and working conditions of child labourers and house-maids.

A study of regional rural bank—their role in rural development.

- Accounting as a tool of resource mobilisation and allocation in developing economy.
- Study of unorganised rural markets—rural markets as an integral feature of rural economy.
- Comparative evaluative study of performance in professionally managed and family run enterprises.
- Liquidity analysis through ratio and cash flow in some industries.